Inc.
MAGAZINE

301

DO-IT-YOURSELF
MARKETING IDEAS

from America's
Most Innovative Small Companies

INTRODUCTION BY JAY CONRAD LEVINSON

EDITED BY SAM DECKER

301
DO-IT-YOURSELF MARKETING IDEAS

301
DO-IT-YOURSELF
MARKETING IDEAS

Nearly half of the ideas in *301 Do-It-Yourself Marketing Ideas* were compiled from original interviews and submissions from successful business managers. The other half was culled from some of *Inc.* magazine's best marketing stories of the last several years. Reading and editing *Inc.* articles, and then finding and arranging original stories, required more effort than I imagined. Technology helped to research, edit, and organize the material. But it was the ideas, effort, and inspiration of several great people who made the biggest contribution to *301 Do-It-Yourself Marketing Ideas.*

In lieu of a book dedication, I give sincere appreciation to my bright and beautiful wife, Shannon, who improved my editing and put up with me working late. Big thanks to several friends who contributed time, contacts, editing skills, and suggestions to this book: Greg Tutton, Fred Loetterle, Liz Seegert, John Leighty, Kara and Kevin Dueck, Lori Walker, Randy Young, Victor and Suzanne Lee, Dru Scott, Chris Edwards, Bob Katz, and Jane Van Suan. I acknowledge my mentors who inspired my marketing and authoring ventures: Bert Decker (my father), Guy Kawasaki, Terri Lonier, and special thanks to Jay Conrad Levinson who wrote the introduction.

I am grateful to the hundreds of business managers who returned my calls, e-mails, and faxes to share their stories. And I appreciate the efforts of the original reporters, editors, and writers of the *Inc.* material: Margherita Altobelli, Christopher Bergonzi, Alessandra Bianchi, Leslie Brokaw, Paul Brown, Bo Burlingham, Christopher Caggiano, Karen Carney, John Case, Elizabeth Conlin, Michael Cronin, Susan Donovan, Tom Ehrenfeld, Donna Fenn, Jay Finegan, Jill Andresky Fraser, David

Freedman, Elyse Friedman, Robina Gangemi, George Gendron, Vera Gibbons, Susan Greco, Stephanie Gruner, Phaedra Hise, Michael Hopkins, Joshua Hyatt, John Kerr, Joel Kotkin, Nancy Lyons, Joshua Macht, Robert Mamis, Martha Mangelsdorf, Cheryl McManus, Anne Murphy, Bruce Posner, Teri Lammers Prior, Tom Richman, Sarah Schafer, Brac Selph, Ellyn Spragins, Edward Welles, Rusty Weston, David Whitford, and Stephanie Zacharek.

Special thanks to the *Inc.* Business Resources(IBR) team, who brought 301 *Do-It-Yourself Marketing Ideas* to life: product director Jan Spiro, who approached me with the book idea; editorial director Bradford W. Ketchum, Jr., who gave me the chance to write it; fact checkers Simeon R. Ketchum and Jason Y. Wood, who made every story accurate; copy editors Jacqueline Lapidus and Diane Bernard, who made the book easy to read; product manager Kate Titus, who managed the production details; and creative director Cynthia M. Davis and design director Kyle Hoepner of Cambridge Prepress Services, for their continued excellence in shaping the 301 series look; *Inc.* executive editor Jeffrey Seglin, who conceived the idea of collecting the best from *Inc.;* Sara Noble, who ran with the idea; designers Robert Lesser and Brady & Paul Communications, for their original book design; and IBR managing editor Sarah T. Johnson, who orchestrated its overall creation.

—*Sam Decker*
Editor
Scotts Valley, Calif.

One good marketing idea is a very precious commodity. One good marketing idea that you can implement all by yourself is equally desirous. Imagine yourself with not only one good marketing idea but 301 of them. Then picture yourself able to breathe life into not just one of those ideas but all 301 of them.

It's enough to make your competitor's mind boggle. It's enough to put a grin from here to Timbuktu on the face of your accountant. And it's enough to fuel your marketing strategy—and your profits—to the point where you can reach and then surpass your goals.

Will any one of these ideas propel you to your goals? Maybe not, but a combination of them will give your business the marketing zest and momentum it needs to satisfy customers and attract prospects.

As all guerrilla marketers know, you are in three businesses at once. One of them, to be sure, is the business you know you're in. Another one is the people business, because that's who will be buying what you're selling. And the third is the marketing business—because it's marketing that's going to motivate people to buy from you.

These days, the brute force of technology is giving small businesses an advantage. They're able to appear as credible and as professional as the big guys without having to spend the big bucks. They can create and produce newsletters and brochures rapidly, inexpensively, and all by themselves. They can become online superstars. And now they can tap into the kind of information that's in this book and cash in on the success of others.

Some of the marketing ideas in this book are simple concepts, such as making sure that every frontline employee in your company asks new customers the six magic words, "How did you hear about us?" Guerrilla

marketers well know that while some marketing weapons hit the bullseye, others miss the target, and the only way to tell the difference is to *ask*.

You'll also discover in these pages treasure troves of new profits from do-it-yourself marketing ideas as mundane as knowing what kind of message to leave on somebody else's voice mail to ensure a return call, and what to say on your own voice mail to make callers feel good.

Did you know how much marketing power a P.S. has at the end of a direct-mail letter? You'll not only learn about the power, but how to tap into it within the pages of this book. Is it really possible to attract 30 to 40 customers a day without spending a dime to attract them? Included is the account of a woman who announced, "We accept competitor coupons," and then reaped a harvest. Simple ideas, all of them. But if they're so simple, why don't most people know them?

The answer is that most people are just plain intimidated by marketing, so they shy away from it rather than make a mistake. This book makes it possible for you to cozy up to marketing with no fear of making a mistake—for others have gone to school for you and now you can benefit from their education, thanks to Sam Decker and *Inc.* magazine.

Do-it-yourself marketing. The guerrilla entrepreneurs of the world owe a tip of their hats to the creators of this book for making their lives easier with this extraordinary compilation of marketing ideas that *can* work, *have* worked, and *will* work.

Jay Conrad Levinson is the author of the Guerrilla Marketing *series of best-selling marketing books. His newest book is* The Way of the Guerrilla, *(Houghton Mifflin, 1997).*

I

"Never write an advertisement which you wouldn't want your family to read. You wouldn't tell lies to your own wife. Don't tell them to mine."

DAVID OGILVY
Ogilvy & Mather advertising agency

IDEA

Take a Flyer

Street marketing can be a cost-effective alternative to conventional television, print, and direct-mail advertising—especially if there's a good reason for people to read the flyers.

Boston's Kung-Fu Tai-Chi Club **relies on flyers to publicize its women's self-defense class**. "Rather than be on page 20 of some little newspaper section, where people might not see us, we're on the street, actively promoting," says co-owner Yao Li.

The small ads he used to place in local papers and magazines, at a cost of $150 to $200 a week, produced a 2% to 5% response at best. So, Li tried a grassroots approach. Students of the Kung-Fu Tai-Chi Club spend two hours distributing 500 flyers in exchange for a free session. Li credits the flyers with 90% of his class enrollment today. "We were going to run one class every six weeks," he says, "but now we have one class every two weeks."

2
IDEA

Community Access Channels

Most cable TV systems set aside a channel for community and non-profit groups to broadcast local events, feature stories, and government meetings. Dave Cioffi, general manager of the 28,000-square-foot Dartmouth Bookstore in Hanover, N.H., found his company could **buy time on a local channel by becoming a sponsor**.

Dartmouth became a "Corporate Leader" sponsor of the channel. For $2,500 a year, a television crew came out and shot a 20-second infomercial for the bookstore, which was broadcast several times each day. In addition, they let Dave and his staff host a weekly 20-minute show featuring Dartmouth's latest books. Sometimes, if the station was short on program content, it ran the same show 10 to 20 times a week. Dartmouth's company logo and tag line were also broadcast 12 times a day, or 4,380 times per year, as a "thanks to our sponsors" message.

"You can't buy this much TV exposure anywhere else for that price," said Cioffi. "We didn't track the response, but we knew people came in all the time asking for the books we featured on the show."

3
IDEA

Ad Analysis

You'd probably pull an ad for a product that wasn't paying for itself, but it's more complicated than that when every ad plugs multiple products.

Tool King, a $7-million specialty retailer chain in Denver, Colo., spends over $600,000 annually in newspaper advertising, each ad promoting several products. Managing partner Donald Cohen **uses his computer to track and analyze the return on his advertisements**. He uses the data to determine what items to advertise and how much space to allot to each.

At the end of each business day, the computer prints a sales analysis that lists the quantities of goods sold in each of Tool King's six stores, total sales per product, profit and cost per product, and total cost per ad per product. Ads are changed daily to reflect the previous day's report. If an ad doesn't pull its weight, Tool King makes a change. If it sees a trend in buying, it gives the items more space. As a result, Cohen notes, his ads resemble "a hit parade of items."

IDEA

Track the (Phone) Numbers

Richard A. Gagne, D.D.S., with an office in Oxnard, Calif., never used to be sure which of the many places he advertised his Adult and Implant Dentistry were generating the most dollars. Then he started **listing different phone numbers in different ads** that were running concurrently. Now he knows which ads are drawing phone calls, compares response rates to ads in different publications, and allocates his budget accordingly.

Gagne's business has four incoming lines—one for general use, one for its old Yellow Pages ad, and two for other ads. When people call his third line, for example, he knows they are responding to his ad in the *L.A. Times.* New calls are entered into a computer system with a referral code. Then the data are merged with the accounting system to determine his return on investment.

Gagne's tracking system has made him a savvy marketer and saved his dental practice money. "We saw our Yellow Pages ad response diminish four years ago, so we got out," says Gagne. "Our competitors are just now realizing the same thing." Gagne has been able to determine a four-to-one return on his ads. He also discovered that an ad with an 800 number will pull 30% more than the same ad with a local number.

What if you only have one or two phone lines? Use extension numbers. As several other small businesses have discovered, extensions work just as well in this case.

Irresistible Bait

In every shipment of her company's product, specialty real-estate appraisal forms, Ruth Lambert enclosed a plastic fishing worm. Talk about **making an impression on customers**! And it worked—they bit.

Lambert's 15-year-old company was the biggest in its field, not to mention one of the world's largest users of plastic fishing worms. The company's slogan: "There's nothing funny about our service." And its name, Forms & Worms Inc., in itself was a stroke of genius, as a leading advertising executive once observed when he saw the name on a list of participants in a conference he was addressing. "Before I start," he said from the podium, "I would like to tell whoever you are from Forms & Worms, and whatever it is you do, don't ever change your name!"

6
IDEA

Extraordinary Exposure

With hundreds of **non-traditional advertising vehicles** at your fingertips these days, at least a handful must cut through the clutter. But when customers are bombarded with hundreds of advertising messages each day, something offbeat and out of the ordinary may be your best bet. Here are some "unique techniques": Place snappy ads...

- Where groups congregate: Ads in schools, health clubs, and bowling alleys; on call-in and on-line information services; in malls, and inside golf-course holes.
- In front of captive audiences: Ads on the telephone while on hold, on airport scheduling screens, restrooms, cinemas, phone booths; or near theme-park lines.
- In stores: Messages on aisle directories, in-store videos, carts, refrigerators, bicycle racks outside—and taped ads mixed with music.
- Any place within customers' view: ATM receipts, vending machines, taxis, trucks, floppy disks, video boxes, and on indoor mini-blimps. Or there's the new talking poster, which senses passersby and plays a recorded message. What's next? One company is testing slogan-decorated eggs—and another is planning ads on hot dog skins.

"Consumers have a composite portrait of a product. By fragmenting media strategies, a product's image becomes fragmented. It is essential for a brand to maintain a consistent face in every aspect of the media: in classical advertising, at point of purchase, through mailings, or even touch screen interactive shopping...Advertising so interrupting, so daring, so fresh, so engaging, so human, so believable and so well-focused as to themes and ideas that, at one and the same time, it builds a quality reputation for the long haul as it produces sales for the immediate present."

LEO BURNETT
Leo Burnett advertising agency

IDEA

Take Me to the Zoo

Know your audience—that's the key to successful do-it-yourself advertising, and it unlocked success for Majda Fiecko, president of the Hair-Do Zoo, children's haircut specialists in Winnipeg, Canada. At Fiecko's two salons, kids have their hair cut while "riding" colorful plastic animals, rather than sitting in traditional barber's chairs. The salon's ad agency was spending twice what was budgeted and was headed in the wrong direction. When Fiecko fired the agency and tackled the job herself on a $12,000 annual marketing budget, she found out the expensive way that her target market was not mothers with children but the children themselves.

Originally Fiecko aired a TV spot during programming aimed at women, with so-so results. But, she said, response went wild when the ad aired during children's programming. One mother rushed her young son to the shop right after seeing the spot, to take advantage of the boy's first-time enthusiasm for a haircut.

Fiecko backs up her TV pitch with flyer campaigns, monthly ads in neighborhood papers, and sponsorship of kid-related community events. "Once you've got those customers, it's all word-of-mouth after that," she says. Now franchising plans are on track, new Hair-Do Zoos are set to open, and the company is planning its own line of children's hair-care products.

8

IDEA

Rear Window

Potential customers are everywhere, even in your rear-view mirror. So why not **advertise your company on vanity license plates**?

Linda Hall Gillen promoted her math tutoring services by personalizing her automobile license plate to read "MATH2TR." Although only seven parents have approached her with requests for help in the five years she's had the plate, the return on investment is still great.

The revenue from these jobs more than paid for the cost of the vanity plate. And Gillen believes it has helped establish her credibility and spread word-of-mouth advertising. Word must be spreading—a couple of years after she obtained the plate she saw a copycat car in her home town with one that read "2TRMATH."

9

IDEA

Wean Yourself from Your Agency

If you're not ready to tackle your advertising campaign by yourself, **split responsibilities with an advertising agency to reduce your marketing costs**. With the help of RDA International—an advertising agency in New York City— Ken Currier, CEO of Expert Software based in Coral Gables, Fla., set up an in-house department to produce advertising pieces RDA developed. Here are some tips on how to make this uncommon arrangement work:

- *Get to know each other.* To learn about Expert's market, RDA attended industry conventions and subscribed to consumer and trade magazines. Meanwhile, Expert invited RDA staffers to attend company functions.
- *Collaborate on strategy.* RDA and Expert determined which marketing pieces were most critical and limited their collaborative effort to package design and sales materials.
- *Bring jobs in-house.* Currier gradually assigned staff to advertising projects and brought manageable projects in-house. RDA advised Expert on equipment and staffing, and designed sample formats to guide staffers. RDA tapered its monthly retainer and continued to provide backup until Expert was on its own.

Four staffers developed marketing strategies, package design, and in-store sales materials for Expert's entertainment software. The cost: $250,000 a year—less than the budget for an external agency. As for the results, Currier pointed to his "Lethal Tender" box design, redone in-house. The software outlived the usual one-year shelf life by five months.

10

IDEA

Humor on Hold

Nobody likes to be put on hold—least of all your customers. To alleviate their frustration, **provide recorded entertainment to callers while they wait**.

Creative Producers Group (CPG), a full-service communications company based in St. Louis, creates off-the-wall, humorous "on-hold" messages that both inform and entertain.

Not only do the tapes entertain the clients, they present CPG's services in an amusing way. "The messages are so enjoyable that callers don't feel like they're getting a sales pitch," says Keith Alper, CPG's president. "A voice-over artist delivers comedy lines mixed with music, and the small investment pays off."

One client, who used Alper's company for video production, learned while on hold that the company also created meeting presentations. When the client was connected, he awarded a new presentation project to CPG. The on-hold messages have not just brought in new business—some clients have even requested copies of the tapes.

II

"I consider it the highest compliment when my employees go out and start their own companies in competition with me. I always send them a plant to wish them well. Of course, it's a cactus."

NORMAN BRODSKY
founder and CEO of Perfect Courier

COMPETITION

11
IDEA

Successful Bidding Secrets

To get new business, most companies chalk up time and energy bidding on customer contracts. However, if you're up against an incumbent, the customer may just be using you to get the competitor's price down. Barry Nalebuff and Adam Brandenburger, authors of *Co-opetition* (Currency/Doubleday, 1996), suggest a couple of ways to **make bidding pay**.

Ask for information. Most companies won't share confidential data, but it doesn't hurt to ask for specifics, such as current costs. The way the customer handles your requests will also tell you whether the company seriously wants to work with you.

Ask to meet others in the company. You don't want to get stuck with someone who cares only about price. You want exposure to as many people in the company as possible; one might become your advocate.

12

IDEA

Misfortune Marketing

When competitors go out of business, don't miss the opportunity to win their customers. One of the best ways to redirect their business to your own is to **have their phone calls forwarded to you**. This tactic worked for Chris Zane, owner of Zane's Cycles, a $1.5-million independent bicycle dealer in Branford, Conn. By offering to pay the local Yellow Pages a small fraction of his defunct competitors' remaining advertising costs, Zane arranged to have their out-of-service phone numbers ring at his shop. The fee was one-third the cost of his competitors' Yellow Pages ads, totalling $200 per month.

Now, when someone calls two of his former competitors, a message states: "The number you are calling is no longer in service. If you are in need of a bicycle dealer, Zane's Cycles will be happy to serve you. To be directly connected toll-free, please press zero now."

The Yellow Pages helped Zane track the transferred calls. He has received 260 inquiries from his competitors' customers in one month. The first day the line was changed, he sold a bike to a customer who had called the defunct competitor.

13
IDEA

Repositioning Your Business

In a competitive market, your company's "position" can determine its success. You define yourself to fit a position in your customers' mind that they believe will meet their needs. At the same time, your position differentiates you from the competition. As market conditions change, however, you may have to change your position to maintain growth.

Andover Controls of Andover, Mass., was a manufacturer of building controls in the 1970s. Employees and customers alike knew they were in the building-controls business, but business wasn't going anywhere. Andover was competing in an emerging market crowded with 350 other climate-control businesses, which became known as "black-box companies." Once management understood this, **the company's story was rewritten to differentiate the business**.

Andover recast itself as being in the "comfort business" and changed its distribution strategy. It paid a higher price for more specialized access to the market, and gave up margin to those distributors who understood its products. Eventually, Andover's products proved to integrate themselves better into the overall mechanics of office buildings. As a result, business took off, and the company surpassed the competition.

Of the 350 "black-box" manufacturers, says Bob Klein, Andover's vice-president of sales, there are no more than 40 still in business. Andover Controls, with $60 million in sales in the United States and Europe and currently expanding in Asia, is among the five largest.

Sharing with Competitors

Faraway competitors really aren't competitors at all, if you serve local markets. However, they understand how to market effectively to your target customers. So why not **exchange tips with similar businesses** to help you both succeed?

Tom Sinclair, owner of HomePro of Alabama, a home inspection service, realized that a "competitor" 60 miles away posed few threats to his local business. He learned that the owner of HomePro of Northwest Florida was willing to brainstorm with him on business ideas, and even to cooperate to penetrate a shared business territory.

After a few meetings, the two home inspectors developed new marketing techniques to attract local business, and built relationships with real-estate agents in an overlapping area neither had considered before because of distance.

Business has picked up for both of them, and sharing business has worked out well. One of the agents in their "shared" area even put them on his local TV show to give home repair advice. The next day, Tom's new partner got a call from someone who saw the show. Since his partner had another appointment, Tom took the inspection.

"Goodwill is the only
asset that competition cannot
undersell or destroy."

MARSHALL FIELD
businessman and philanthropist

15
IDEA

Keeping Tabs on the Competition

Finding out what your rivals are up to is one of the trickiest tasks of running a business. Most companies gather intelligence by talking to their salespeople and customers and by reading industry publications. Collecting promotional literature and **putting competitors to an actual test** are ways to expand the scrutiny.

Joe Lethert, president of Performark, a provider of incentive services, based in Minneapolis, maintained a library of competitors' materials so he could quickly compare his prices with those of 8 or 10 competitors, whose catalogs might list from 500 to 5,000 items each. To encourage the sales force to collect rivals' selling materials, Lethert paid his employees $35 for each new piece of competitor's literature they brought in.

When Richard Skeie was CEO of CE Software Holdings, in West Des Moines, Iowa, he bought the competition's software, tested it, and called rivals' tech support, checking their answers for speed, accuracy, and friendliness.

And Pamela Kelley, founder of lace curtain cataloger Rue de France, in Newport, R.I., put in "tricky, horrible orders" to competitors to see how they handled them.

16

IDEA

Carpe Diem Means Seize Customers

When your competitor snubs its own customers, seize the day— or in Latin, *carpe diem*. That's what small banks did when Bank of America (BofA) acquired Security Pacific in 1993.

To consolidate its operations, BofA started closing 450 Security Pacific branches. "We saw this merger as a once-in-a-lifetime opportunity," said Dennis Shireley, then marketing director for First Interstate Bank of California. His bank, and others like it, **used guerrilla marketing tactics to capture customers** who would find banking with BofA less desirable.

Redlands Federal Bank in Redlands, Calif., posted 25 billboards that read, "Lost your sense of Security?" Employees from Sanwa Bank set up sidewalk card tables across the street from closing branches. Bank of Fresno started promoting free checking accounts for seniors because BofA had dropped the program after the merger.

17
IDEA

Coupon Espionage

Battling competitors with coupons can get expensive. You pay for printing and distribution, battle for exclusivity in advertising, and in the end you sell more for less money. Eventually, customer loyalty is based on the deal of the day, and profits erode.

Heather Louis, owner of Yogurt Express in Capitola, Calif., experienced the pitfalls of coupon warfare. When she opened her doors, she was already couponing to acquire new customers. After about a year, she got fed up with matching competitors' coupon discounts and turned the tables. She stopped issuing coupons altogether and started **using competitors' advertising to her advantage** by offering to accept their coupons.

Louis advertises "We accept competitor coupons" in newspapers, on a sign in her store, and through word of mouth. She's happy with the results: Yogurt Express accepts between 30 to 40 coupons per day, all of them distributed by its competitors.

Sole Sponsor

Few things are more fun than **taking the limelight from your competitor**. And at A.C. Petersen Farms, an ice cream manufacturer and restaurant chain in West Hartford, Conn., everything is about having fun.

One summer, a local high school asked Allen Petersen, owner of the family-run company, if he would donate ice cream for a party celebrating the incoming class of 2000. The administrator rattled off a list of participating food sponsors, including a dessert co-sponsor, Friendly Ice Cream. Petersen pointed out that if she had called him first, he would have personally served the entire class with an ice cream sundae cart. Would he really do this? Petersen responded, "I will if Friendly is not there!"

The surprised administrator asked if she could call Petersen back. Ten minutes later she did, asking if it would be all right if Friendly donated five gallons of milk. Petersen agreed.

The next day a reporter wanted to know all about Petersen's generous donation. The article appeared on the front page of the *West Hartford News* the following week. The ice cream was a hit, and Petersen's total cost was under $100. "But the good will could not have been bought," he adds. "Six months later, people were still thanking me for the party!" No one even touched the five gallons of milk donated by his competitor.

"If you fail to plan for competitive pressure, you risk falling into the gas-station-price-war mentality. When you do that, you may find yourself responding to other moves by competitors, rather than taking the initiative yourself. Essentially, you are letting the competition determine your marketing strategy."

DAVID E. GUMPERT
How to Really Create a Successful Marketing Plan
(*Inc.*, 3rd edition, 1996)

19
IDEA

Sharing the Wealth

Competitors can be good for your business, believes Richard Gottschneider, president of RKG Associates, a $1.5-million real-estate consulting firm in Durham, N.H. He gets job referrals by **sending his company newsletter to his rivals**.

The semiannual four-page newsletter features items on RKG Associates projects, regional news, and economic issues. It costs about 25 cents per newsletter to produce and mail to some 2,000 current and prospective clients and 50 competitors. The first two national mailings brought two jobs and lots of leads from competitors. "We refer work to them and they do the same for us. There is more than enough work to go around," says Gottschneider.

20
IDEA

All "Fore" Speed

In today's fast-moving world, there's one aspect of your business you should look at to **gain a competitive advantage: speed**.

Faster delivery was the goal of Spalding Sports Worldwide's Top-Flite Custom Golf Ball division, which produces quality golf balls that customers use as popular business gifts, employee rewards, and trade-show giveaways. Imprinted with a company's logo, the balls are a fun and affordable present with long-time recognition value.

Many corporate planners are professional procrastinators, however, and ordering custom golf balls may be the last thing on their to-do lists. Standard delivery time for similar orders from other companies runs about four weeks, making it difficult for corporate buyers to plan effectively for many events. So, Top-Flite introduced five-day shipment on all orders. For serious procrastinators who can't wait even a week, the company offers one-day express service.

Top-Flite scored a hole-in-one with its speedy service, significantly increasing its market share and racking up thousands of additional logo golf-ball orders.

21

IDEA

Ask Your Competitors for New Business

New kids on the block can easily charm the competition—just **volunteer to take on the overflow work** that established firms can't handle.

Gordon F. Currie, a Web design consultant in Dawson Creek, British Columbia, was looking to build his business and expand into the United States. He accomplished his goal by forming freelance relationships, working with, rather than against, the U.S.-based competition.

First Currie searched the Web for others offering Web design services. He visited these competitors' sites, found an e-mail address, and sent them an honest, modest letter advising that he was available for overflow work. Few responded negatively, and many sent him thanks for keeping his solicitation short, polite, and focused.

Currie's targeted e-mail went out to about 600 companies. Of those, 190 responded, and about 40 competitors requested his rates. Of those, three have sent him work. These three competitors (one in New York, two in California) now account for over 80% of Currie's Web work.

III

> "People expect a certain reaction from a business, and when you pleasantly exceed those expectations, you've somehow passed an important psychological threshold."

RICHARD THALHEIMER
president, The Sharper Image

22 IDEA

Tune In to TV

Seminars can be an effective way to sell a complex product, service, or contract. One of the difficulties, however, is preparing and delivering compelling content to attract attendees. So, instead of developing his own seminar, Drew Santin's company **tuned in to a satellite-broadcast educational show and invited his prospects and customers to watch**.

Santin Engineering, in West Peabody, Mass., helps manufacturers build prototypes. Its technologies and capabilities were complex and difficult to explain to new prospects. When Santin learned that his trade association was transmitting a conference on using technology to make prototypes rapidly—which described his services—he took advantage of the opportunity. For a $400 fee paid to the conference producers, Santin transformed his $4-million company into an authorized viewing site. For another $700, which included installation and set-up, he rented a satellite dish for one day. The 50-employee company sent out press releases about the telecast. Customers and prospects who came to watch the seminar were treated to a buffet lunch and company tour.

Santin considered his in-house seminar a success. Of an estimated 60 people in attendance, half were new customers. After the broadcast, Santin addressed any questions his audience had raised, getting to know them personally. Also, the press releases resulted in several interviews by local radio and cable stations, raising the profile of his 40-year-old family business.

23
IDEA

Zealot Club

How do you start a core of evangelists for your business? **Turn enthusiastic customers into experts and zealots for your products.**

Janene Centurione, who operates two Great Harvest Bread bakeries, a $1.75-million business in Ann Arbor and Birmingham, Mich., spends virtually all of her marketing budget enlisting loyal customers to spread the word about the company's bread. She and her 50 employees look for enthusiastic patrons who ask lots of questions about the products, and ask those customers to join, for free, the "bread zealot" club.

In effect, Centurione turns her zealots into bread experts who want to share their knowledge with others. Each month she sends out to almost 7,000 zealots (about 20% of her clientele) postcards that share information, such as bread recipes. Zealots receive early notices about new product releases, along with the occasional 10%-off coupon. When new customers come in asking about a new bread, she knows it is a referral because the only place she mentions new products is on the zealot postcards.

Centurione estimates that the annual cost of keeping customers in the know comes to about $7 a head, but each recruit to the club brings in about $200 a year. She contrasts that with the $80 a year she spent on bringing in each new customer when she relied solely on traditional advertising. In two years, per-visit sales have climbed from $4.75 to $8.75, which she believes is directly attributable to an increased awareness of her products. Simultaneously, net sales grew 18% a year for the first three years of the zealot club, while the number of zealots has increased almost tenfold.

Automatic Orders

Encourage low-cost ordering and automate customer service by **implementing an interactive voice response system (IVR)**. Callers use their telephone keypads to enter item numbers, a customer-identification number from a catalog or other identifier, and credit-card information. A recorded voice confirms the information they enter and generates a packing list for the warehouse staff.

Christian Book Distributors (CBD), which has 270 employees and 14,000 titles, installed a new automated system from Syntellect, in Phoenix, for $90,000. The system can handle 24 calls concurrently.

"About 15% of the company's phone-in customers choose the automated system," says co-founder Ray Hendrickson. Given that these orders would cost him $1.50 to $2 per order in live operator costs, he estimates the system paid for itself in eight months.

25
IDEA

Easier with E-mail

As more and more people prefer communication by e-mail, the face of customer service is changing. If you are considering e-mail but haven't taken the next step, consider the advantages reported by these companies.

Checkfree, a Columbus, Ohio, electronic-bill payment company, receives two-thirds of its customer-service questions via e-mail since encouraging customers to use it. Customers can ask why a check was posted a day early and receive a reply within 24 hours.

E-mail connection was crucial for Nancy Goodfellow, an account executive at Libby Perszyk Kathman, a Cincinnati package-design firm. When a major client requested a quick turnaround on uncontracted work, Goodfellow quickly e-mailed a proposed budget to the client's staff, and within 24 hours they had approved it.

Joe Boxer, the San Francisco clothing company, deals with retail buyers although it has no consumer catalog, using the Internet to reach its younger fans. The e-mail address (joeboxer@jboxer.com) is on the clothing hang tag and on billboards. Because so many have requested a catalog, marketing chief Denise Slattery says that at some point she will go back to management and say, "Okay, it's time."

United Lithographers, a commercial printer in Spokane, Wash., can **return accurate job quotes in rapid response by e-mail**. Sales manager Chris Snider explains, "When we receive a customer's instructions, we simply insert the price and the purchase-order number and send it back as confirmation."

26
IDEA

Friendly Voice Mail

Press one if you'd like to leave a message..." Sound familiar? Electronic voice-mail messages can alienate your customers, suppliers, and associates—but it doesn't have to be that way. To "connect" with your caller, **record a personal, light-hearted message** that is updated every day or week.

Jerry Greenfield, of Ben & Jerry's Homemade Ice Cream, uses a voice-mail message that reflects his customer-friendly philosophy. Here's an example of one of Greenfield's messages: "Hi, this is Jerry. How ya doing? Hey, thanks for calling. Uh. I'll be in on Tuesday, starting at about 10 or so, hanging out for the day. I won't be in on Wednesday. I'll be in Thursday some of the time. And I won't be in on Friday. And then Saturday and Sunday I will be at the Ben and Jerry's One World, One Heart Festival, at Sugarbush, Vt.... Free! Incredible. Five-dollar parking charge. Carpool. Bring all your friends. Come say hi. I'll be there. I can't wait. If you need to speak to a person... hit zero. Otherwise, you can leave me a message. Hope everything's good. See you. Bye."

27
IDEA

Mail Bonding

Two keys to earn repeat business from customers are: keep in touch with them and encourage them to use your products. BayWare, makers of a Japanese language software tutorial, **used registration cards and postcard support to build its customer relationships**.

Andrew Wang, co-founder of the $1.5-million software company in San Mateo, Calif., dropped a postcard twice a month to customers who purchased his tutorial. The neon-colored cards regaled the users (many of them business travelers) with tips on Japanese customs and pronunciation, printed in English and Japanese.

The cards kept coming for a year—but only after a customer returned the registration card. During the software installation a message flashes, listing the rewards for registering. Some 60% of customers responded, about twice the norm.

Mailing out 5,000 postcards every other week was a job for BayWare's eight-person staff, but the cost (about $2,400 per month to produce and mail) paled next to the payoff. "The purpose was to keep the language alive and keep in touch with customers," said Wang. "It's also turned out to be great for marketing."

28
IDEA

Over-the-Top Customer Service

Pushing the limits of customer service may not be part of your marketing plan. It's not a tactic. It is a philosophy, a principle, and an attitude that your whole company must share for it to work. And when it works, it can pay off.

Stew Leonard's, the Norwalk, Conn., milk-delivery business that grew into a $200-million grocery business, **encourages employees to use initiative to satisfy customers**. One Saturday a woman came in to order $40 worth of food for a lunch party of 20. The chef told her she really should order more, but she resisted. A few hours later the manager got a frantic phone call. "Why didn't you insist I buy more food? I'm going to run out!" The manager put together another $40 tray, drove it over to her house, and apologized. He also refused payment, saying, "No, it's on us."

It turned out that the party was for 20 real estate agents new to the area. "Now, what's the first thing someone who's buying a house wants to know? Where's the grocery store!

"Right after their party all 20 came down to the store and bought hundreds and hundreds of dollars' worth of food—they all had full shopping carts," recalls Stew Leonard Jr., president of his family's business.

"One of the unique things we small companies have over the big guys is the ability to establish personal relationships. Big companies really can't do that. You read about effective organizations, learning organizations, lean and mean organizations, but small companies can be virtuous organizations. It's really hard to think of a huge company being called virtuous. We as small companies can have virtue because we as small companies are basically the embodiment of one or two people, and people can have virtue, while organizations really can't."

JIM KOCH
founder of Boston Beer Company,
maker of Sam Adams beer

29
IDEA

Something Extra

Want to wow customers? Then **do a little something extra**, unexpected, or unique. Simple efforts like these can build word-of-mouth advertising and keep customers coming back:

- A Straw Hat Pizza in Capitola, Calif., lets the kids ride the motorized pony for free.
- Larry's Shoes, a chain of men's shoe stores in Fort Worth, Texas, gives its customers foot massages while the salesperson searches for the right shoe size.
- A plumber in Phoenix gives each customer a small bottle of liquid drain cleaner after a house call.
- Chili's Grill and Bar post the daily sports page above the men's bathroom urinals.

30
IDEA

Byte the Bagels

Large companies have been using sophisticated computer systems to track customers and analyze consumer feedback for a long time. Now more small and midsize companies are enlisting technology to press an advantage in **personalized service and focused marketing**.

Boston-based bagel chain Finagle A Bagel used to keep track of weekly suggestion and complaint calls with Post-It Notes. But the $9.5-million company was expanding rapidly, and director of marketing Heather Robertson was concerned that an increase in caller volume would lead to some calls slipping between the cracks. Larry Smith, founder and president, decided it was time for a customer-comment database.

Now, every time a customer calls, Robertson records his or her name, phone number, and comments. If that customer calls again, she can retrieve the data and talk as though every detail of the last call is fresh in her mind. "That sort of service can turn an angry customer into a fanatically loyal one," she says.

Managers can sort through the database to identify problems and fix them. One guy kept complaining that the salt bagels weren't salty enough, although the database indicated he was alone in his sentiments. Robertson's solution: Given 24 hours' notice, Finagle would have a dozen extra-salty bagels waiting for the finicky customer at the nearest shop. "People can get very vocal about their bagels," Robertson says. "We have to let them know we're listening."

31
IDEA

Little Gifts Mean a Lot

Successful gift-giving builds relationships with clients. And for Brooks-Pollard Company, a marketing consulting firm in Little Rock, Ark., nothing works better than **giving clients a personal letter and a gift to show appreciation**.

Every Thanksgiving, CEO Hugh Hart Pollard writes a personal "thank-you" letter to clients and sends it to their homes. Each letter describes the individual relationship he has with his clients and lets them know how important they are to him, not only professionally, but personally.

With each letter Pollard sends a book matched to the customer's personal interest, such as art, entertaining, or sailing. Customers usually write or call to thank Pollard for the gift. The book/letter combination strengthens the personal relationship, makes his customers feel important, and encourages them to approach him with any issues.

32

IDEA

For Whom the Toll's Free

When you call a company, you don't want to hear "That's not my department; let me put you on hold" on your dime. So, Deck House Inc., a company in Acton, Mass., that designs and manufactures prefabricated post-and-beam houses, **dedicated an 800 line to inquiring potential and current customers**. Once callers are satisfied, the $20-million company keeps them on the line to conduct market research and get customer histories and referrals. To make sure customers use the line, CEO Michael Harris sends them plastic wallet cards touting the Deck House Owner Assistance Center, with the 800 number.

By the end of the customer-service line's first year, 2,018 calls had come in. Twenty-three percent of the 800-line callers wanted to buy something, and 10% required other sales information; 17% asked maintenance questions; 12% asked miscellaneous questions. Fewer than 15% of the calls were complaints.

An 800 number might be a luxury for most small manufacturers, but Deck House depends on repeat business and referrals for 40% of its business. About one in four callers are willing to pass on names of friends who might like to receive literature from Deck House; those referrals lead to a sale nearly every month.

"Avoid mass promotion. We have some common material that we give each customer, but we also tailor each package to address their specific needs. It's more important to understand the markets you want to serve, then go out and find the matches."

PAUL STANFIELD
operations manager, ABCO Automation, Inc.
Browns Summit, N.C.

33
IDEA

'Tis Another Season

There was a time when sending Christmas cards was an effective way to plant your company's name before current and prospective customers. "People can't help feeling warmly about you," says Jack Kahl, chairman of Manco, a $180-million marketer of tapes, weather stripping, and mail supplies. But, says Kahl, there is only so much warmth to go around.

So many companies now send holiday cards that yours can get lost in the shuffle. To break through, he has **added less popular holidays to his greeting card mailing roster**: Thanksgiving, St. Patrick's Day, and the Fourth of July, to be specific.

To heighten interest, he has the cards designed in-house so they're different from run-of-the-mill greetings. "People open them up just to see what the next one will look like," says Kahl, whose mailing list includes some 32,000 people. "It's a much more personal way to reach them."

34
IDEA

It's the President Calling

Some customers out there are simply afraid to complain—they'd rather switch companies than fight. But dissatisfied customers can wreak havoc on repeat business and word-of-mouth advertising.

Clarke Otten, president of Professional Swedish Car Repair in Atlanta, ferreted out problems by **telephoning all customers** one week after they visited either of his two locations. He set aside an hour or two a day to make 20 to 50 calls.

Customers remembered that the president of the company called them, and they really felt serviced. Otten got them to admit what was bothering them and addressed their problems right on the spot. The calls also kept his 12 employees on their toes. They knew the boss was in touch with the front line and wouldn't let anything slip by.

35
IDEA

Sunniest Home Videos

We'd lecture employees all day long about what needed to be improved, and they wouldn't get it," recalls Mark Taylor, CEO of AFS Window & Door, a $10-million manufacturer based in Anaheim, Calif. So, Taylor held meetings every two months and served pizza to his 70 employees while they watched videos—videos of AFS's customers at construction sites pointing out problems with the windows.

Since the **customer video sessions** began, complaints were cut by more than 60%, and returns due to poor shipping and handling became rare. Salespeople, who doubled as camera-crew members, reported that customers were flattered to have their complaints addressed so responsibly. Employees immediately saw how mistakes could cause problems and knew what needed to be done.

Playing for Keeps

Most companies are serious about building customer relationships and loyalty. For American Information Systems (AIS) in Fort Lauderdale, Fla., it was all part of the game—literally. While baseball fans were watching their favorite teams on TV, AIS customers were fielding fly balls batted by AIS employees.

Originally, AIS was a start-up eager to **build customer loyalty** for its integrated telephone and computer systems. Years later, each of AIS's 61 offices had sold customers on a 10-month-season baseball program playing against AIS employee and other customer teams. The top teams played off in a championship series at the New York Yankees' spring-training field in Fort Lauderdale. And AIS picked up the tab for the weekend series. "If they switch vendors, our customers have to turn in their uniforms," said CEO Jack Namer. "They're loyal."

"Would you take a new prospect
into this customer's plant
or offices to show off your
partnership? If you can't get
a good reference from this
account—or if you aren't willing
to ask for one—you need to
re-examine the relationship."

**ROBERT MILLER
AND STEPHEN HEIMAN**
Successful Large Account Management
(Warner Books, 1991)

37
IDEA

Back-Office Service Up Front

A surefire way to prove your commitment to customer service is to **send your back-office people into the field to complement your sales force**.

Shepard Poorman Communications, a printing company in Indianapolis, routinely sent its hands-on workers to meet with the editors whose manuscripts it handled.

According to Don Curtis, vice president for quality, the payoff was terrific. Press workers may not be slick salespeople, but they solved problems for customers who weren't aware the problems existed. "Customers were grateful, operations were more efficient, and product quality improved," said Curtis.

Proactive Refund from G.O.D.

When guaranteed service falls short, don't just offer a money-back guarantee—**send customers their refunds even before they ask for them**.

G.O.D. (Guaranteed Overnight Delivery), a Kearny, N.J., overnight express-freight company, made its customers' day. Using a customer service strategy, not only did it send accounting departments invoices, it also sent purchasing agents reports detailing the previous month's deliveries and dates missed (if any), with a refund check made out to purchasing. Why not just send the check to accounting? "Because the people who process the billing don't decide which company to use," said CEO Walter Riley.

G.O.D.'s itemized reports really impressed purchasers, who 99% of the time didn't even know they were due a refund. A report and check were relatively simple for G.O.D. to generate but would require a lot of legwork for purchasers to produce. As a result of G.O.D.'s efforts, the purchasers looked better upstairs and remained loyal customers.

39

IDEA

Entertain Customers' Kids

Make the kids happy in your store and the parents are likely to come back. This philosophy has worked for Barbara Fitz, owner of Green Mansions Florist in Centreville, Va.

Fitz put a fish tank and a miniature picnic table in a corner of the store, stocked the area with toys and books, and designated it as the **children's area**. If kids behave themselves, they are treated to free stickers and a flower when they leave.

"When busy parents come to buy flowers after work, the last thing they want to do is corral their children," says Fitz. "This area keeps the kids from knocking over vases while their parents choose bouquets. We want children and parents to have a wonderful experience." In one instance, a father built a block tower with his son while he waited for his order. Experiences like this help families remember her florist shop and keep them coming back.

40
IDEA

Don't Miss a Call

A phone system that keeps customers from hanging up will also keep them coming back. John McManus, CEO of Magellan's, a travel-equipment catalog house in Santa Barbara, Calif., could testify to that.

Each morning his six answering machines used to play back partial orders and messages saying, "I'm not leaving my credit-card number on an answering machine!" He could only guess how many potential customers had hung up.

Then McManus discovered the AT&T Merlin Legend, an **automated answering and order-taking system**, which has voice prompts that ask callers for their name, address, credit-card number, item number, and quantity. He signed a $45,000, five-year contract that covered a dozen phone lines—taking not only calls throughout the night but also overflow calls during the day. That was a good deal, because staffing for the overflow coverage alone would have taken two more employees at a cost of at least $32,000 a year.

The day after the system was installed, McManus knew he'd made the right investment. Previously, Magellan's would receive some 20 messages during the night, mostly catalog requests and "a few brave orders." That morning McManus counted more than 200 messages, with a higher percentage of orders than usual. That ratio has stayed high: Since then about 35% of all calls have been orders, up from 10% during the old answering machine days. And McManus's reorder rate hit an industry high—about 40%.

IDEA

Tailor-Made Customer Service

Does your professional clientele expect more but want to pay less? Are you facing lots of competition? Are new customers too expensive to find?

Here's what one-to-one-marketing gurus Don Peppers and Martha Rogers would do if asked to stand in as CEOs of a hypothetical company, Downtown Deluxe Dry Cleaning.

- **Offer personalized service**. Remember each customer's individual preferences—no starch, folded, or on hangers.
- Learn faces and names, especially of regular clients. Train your counter people.
- When a new customer walks in, ask permission to take a Polaroid snapshot, to help salespeople recognize him or her the next time.
- Write up an inventory of customers' clothes as they acquire them, and keep it current for insurance purposes.
- Offer a used-clothing service for those customers. Appraise and donate customers' used clothing to a charity, then give them the tax receipt.
- Do a variety of "nuisance" errands for customers for a fee per transaction, usually $5 or less: key duplication, shoe shining, and the like.
- Allow customers to provide an extra key to their car door and simply leave their dirty clothes on the back seat. Go by their parking spaces in the company garage once a week or once a day, check the back seat for a pickup, and hang freshly cleaned clothing inside.
- Offer monthly billing, or bill clients' credit cards monthly.

42

IDEA

Education for Extraction

Marc J. Beshar, a 38-year-old dentist with a thriving Manhattan practice, insisted that well-educated customers were key to repeat business. So he used first visits as **one-on-one information sessions to educate his clients**. Could all the information in the world persuade someone to choose a root canal? "You'd be surprised," he said. "I sold high-quality dentistry, and I got people to define how much they valued their teeth."

An hour-long visit gave Beshar the chance to explain his philosophy of dental care to each new patient before he ever touched a tooth. When he asked, "How do you feel about being here?" some answered, "What the hell kind of question is that?" Although he lost some patients and staff when he took an "information, please" approach to dentistry, the practice started to grow. Beshar's loyal patients valued his personal approach and the extras—like a free baby-sitting service. The end result: Word of mouth brought him all the business he needed.

43
IDEA

High-Tech and Personal

A high-tech communication system, no matter how convenient, is no substitute for personal interaction.

When Winguth, Donahue & Co., an executive search firm in Los Altos, Calif., installed a new voice-mail system, clients started complaining it was too cold and annoying. The company lost prospects, clients, and revenue.

Owner Ed Winguth realized that if clients complained so heartily about the phones, he could only imagine what else was on their minds. So he began following up with repeat clients after making a placement. The experience refocused him on staying in touch with customers.

Winguth found a **software program that reminded him to call or write after a job's completion**—for example, on the anniversary date of a client's signing on. This interactive approach enabled Winguth to win back a client who was satisfied with his service but had contracted another because the firm lost touch.

44

IDEA

E-Mail Boosts Service

Faster than faxing and cheaper than phones, **electronic mail is changing the face of customer service**. It certainly did for Communications Marketing and Distribution (CMD), an Atlanta-based company that warehouses promotional materials.

Ten of CMD's 20 largest accounts were hooked directly into CMD's system, allowing them to place orders for items, such as brochures, directly into CMD's system, leaving an electronic paper trail. "Customers could order any time of day and add to their purchase," said CMD president Mark Nedza. Two years since implementing e-mail, CMD's sales tripled and its phone bill dropped from $1,200 to $900 a month.

Twenty CMD staffers used e-mail to process more than 7,000 messages each month, including invoices, purchase orders, supplier updates, reports, and questions. CMD dedicated one person, on $35,000 salary, to manage the e-mail part time. Without the e-mail hookup, CMD estimates it would need at least three more customer-service reps to handle the same business.

45
IDEA

Satisfaction Guaranteed

Here are some tips for **gauging customer satisfaction**:

- Carneiro, Chumney & Co., a San Antonio accounting firm, enclosed a short questionnaire with each invoice. While it saved stamps, there was another reason for sending the survey: "When a customer paid the bill, it was the ultimate evaluation," said managing partner Bob McAdams. Of those who returned the card, only 1% gave Carneiro less than a 4.2 rating on a scale of one to five.

- Classy Chassis, a chain of car washes based in Biloxi, Miss., employed "exit people" who checked quality before customers drove off. Customers of its special detailing services (like hand waxing) were asked to rate performance. "We see 300 to 400 cars a day, so we focused on 10 to 25 at each of our car washes," said owner Tom Wall. Those who filled out a survey got 50% off their next wash.

- Customer comment cards were often served up with dessert, but Chef Allen's, a North Miami Beach restaurant, topped them off with a phone call. "For parties of eight or more, we called the host of the party the following day to make sure it went okay," said owner Allen Susser. "This works well since he or she may not want to complain in front of others, and these hosts tend to be important customers who spend a lot of money."

46
IDEA

Umbilical Cordless

Remember when nobody could reach you while you were traveling or out of the office for an appointment? Now you can **use a cellular phone to stay connected to clients** and staff all the time, anywhere—to the benefit of your business.

To increase customer service and sales, Freestone, Calif.-based building contractor Michael Eschenbach bought a cellular phone. He pays $200 a month for his calls but isn't complaining about the cost.

Indeed, these days he doesn't know how he lived without it. "Clients love having instant access to me 12 hours a day," says Eschenbach. He lands new clients who normally hang up if they receive a recorded message. He can forward "bid calls" that come into the office directly to his cellular phone, then stop by the prospect's site and provide immediate service. In addition to clients finding him when they need him, he's finding more time to get things done.

Eschenbach estimates the phone has helped increase sales by $2,000 a month. He believes full-time availability is a major factor in helping his business grow 30% a year.

47
IDEA

• CUSTOMER RELATIONS •

Mensch Marketing

Personal recommendation is a powerful, often overlooked, low-cost marketing tool that customers trust. It works. And there is no better way to **encourage others to recommend you** than to be a "mensch marketer."

Mensch (a Yiddish word meaning a real person) marketing is letting others know you care about them as people, not merely as customers. Salli Rasberry, marketing consultant in Freestone, Calif., and co-author of *Marketing Without Advertising* (Nolo Press, 2nd edition, Berkeley, Calif.), suggests three ways to do it successfully.

- Acknowledge the accomplishments of colleagues, suppliers, clients, and competitors by sending them greeting cards. Address the envelopes by hand.
- Keep an ongoing file of cartoons and quotes. Fax them to prospective clients and anyone on your mailing list you haven't heard from in a while.
- Call suppliers from time to time and thank them for continuing to give you such good service. Or, pay their bills a little early.

Gestures like these create the best advertising of all—word-of-mouth.

48

IDEA

Every Employee a Sleuth

Next time you prepare a customer-satisfaction survey, ask your employees to anticipate your customers' responses. Have them complete the survey as they think your customers will, then compare the results of both groups. This will tell you how much education or reinforcement is needed to **keep employees attuned to your customers**.

Sybil Stershic, president of Quality Service Marketing in Honesdale, Pa., and a recent chairperson of the American Marketing Association, further suggests finding ways for employees who have no direct customer contact to see customers as real people rather than faceless names or account numbers.

- At staff meetings, discuss various "clues" to customer satisfaction. For example, a restaurant dishwasher can gauge customer satisfaction by observing how much food comes back on the plates.
- Periodically invite non-contact employees to accompany your sales team to customer sites.
- Start an "Adopt-a-Customer" program in which non-contact employees are assigned customers to visit on a quarterly basis.

Stershic also suggests involving employees in brainstorming sessions to uncover their own ideas for connecting with customers. Sensitizing employees at all levels to customer needs is likely to improve service and turn more satisfied customers into repeat business.

49
IDEA

Here Comes Your Product

Something as simple as a **courtesy call** can increase customer goodwill and loyalty. For Best Mailing Lists, a mailing list rental company in Tucson, Ariz., their "friendly shipping call" has become its competitive advantage.

Karen Kirsch, president of the company, believes in superior service. Her philosophy includes calling customers as soon as their mailing list order is shipped to acknowledge shipment and wish them luck on their direct mail campaign. "People really appreciate it," says Kirsch. "It's good-will that is priceless." The tactic also increases business. The call connects the customer with the company again, and often reminds them of lists they will need for their next project. Kirsh says that 50% of her customers give her repeat business.

IV

"As the number of catalogs in the mailbox grows, so does the level of sophistication of the customer. The demands grow on our ingenuity, innovativeness, and imagination to make smarter-looking, better catalogs. Our customers want to see more, and they want to be entertained and sweet-talked. While you're at it, show them something new and different."

JO-VON TUCKER
JVT Direct Marketing and Clambake
Celebrations, Orleans, Mass.

50

IDEA

Putting Business on the Map

If you're having trouble locating prospects and customers, try geographic information systems (GIS). A GIS **takes geographical data from satellites and matches it against relevant business data**.

This technology has worked wonders for Archadeck, based in Richmond, Va. With nearly 80 offices in 24 states, the home-add-on franchise continually searches the nation for clients. Several years ago, the company began managing its direct-contact marketing campaigns with GeoWizard, a GIS "prospect-finder" produced by GeoDemX Corp (810-569-3939).

The director of marketing for Archadeck logged their projects into a GIS database, drew a circle with a fifth-of-a-mile radius around each one, and "asked" GeoWizard to pull out the names and addresses of surrounding homeowners. Before construction of a project, these homeowners were sent a postcard that read: "We're adding a new deck to 100 Chestnut Street, a couple of doors down. Why not come over and have a look?"

Since adopting GIS, Archadeck's direct-mail postcard return rate tripled, and the system paid for itself in just a few years. For a 50,000-address mailing, Archadeck asked GeoWizard for names matching the demographic profile and landscape the company was targeting through its own market research. The program turned up 45,000 likely prospects, saving Archadeck $4,000 in mailing lists.

51
IDEA

Response to Packaging

Ann Withey, owner of Annie's Homegrown, a $3.5 million Sausalito-and Boston-based macaroni-and-cheese manufacturer, boasts a database of 75,000 customer names. How does a company that never sees the customer do that? **The answer is in their packaging. It begs a response**.

First, Annie's encourages word-of-mouth marketing by offering to send discount coupons to customers' friends. Also, Withey puts her Web site address (URL) on the back of the box, which lures almost 400 visitors weekly. She offers free "Be Green" bumper stickers and $1 refrigerator magnets. Annie's Homegrown even publishes her home phone number on the side. "We wanted people to realize there's a real Annie," says Deborah Churchill Luster, president of the company.

Withey, who works from her Connecticut farm, gets about 50 calls a day from customers. She asks callers for feedback about the product and in-store promotions.

"When people pick a package up off the shelf, they don't expect to be talked to," says Luster. "Until recently, the only advertising we did was on the box."

Alternative Mailing Lists

Many businesses get direct-mail lists from list brokers. However, with names costing between $90 to $250 per thousand for one-time use, you may want to build your own database using alternative methods.

Start by capturing the names and addresses of existing customers. One way is to ask for their addresses when they order, or take the information off their check. You could also ask them to fill out a short survey in exchange for a discount or free gift.

To obtain new customer files, collect names and addresses from e-mail "signatures" on Internet discussion boards and e-mail lists. Another great mailing-list resource is Select Phone from Pro CD (800-99-CD-ROM). You can extract just about every company and residential business address in the country from this $99 CD-ROM. Also, swap lists with noncompeting businesses or work out other partnerships to capture new addresses.

Craig Rosen, owner of At Athletic Supply in Dallas, **partnered with big companies to build his mailing list database**. He tried ad inserts in credit-card bills and a special offer with Procter & Gamble. He gave space in his own catalog to GTE's NFL-theme calling card in exchange for the names of buyers GTE obtains from its Super Bowl ads and other venues. His one-year goal: to add 100,000 names to his house list at little cost. After only seven months, he had obtained 75,000 new names for free.

53

IDEA

Mailroom Savings

To stretch your marketing budget this year, head first for the mail-room. "Postage is one of those things that's often overlooked," says Dan Francis, CEO of St. Louis Pre-Sort, a Missouri business that sorts and puts bar codes on mail for 500 corporate clients. He offers these suggestions for **saving on postage**:

- Plan ahead. Mailings that aren't time sensitive can be shipped standard, instead of first class, saving several cents a piece.

- Consider size. If possible, use a standard business envelope instead of a 9-by-12-inch envelope. You'll save several cents per piece, as well, plus the cost of the more expensive envelopes. Mail that has been presorted but doesn't meet post-office size guidelines is slapped with a hefty service charge.

- Clean up your list. Postal Business Centers around the country will perform a onetime free service: they will take your mailing list (up to 50,000 names) and insert the correct standardized addresses. You can also incorporate the bar codes using programs such as Mail Manager 2000, by BCC Software (800-453-3130), or My Professional Mail Manager from My Software Co. (413-473-3600). Either way, you'll probably qualify for the post office's automation discount.

54

IDEA

Newsletter Know-How

van Levison, a direct-mail and advertising copywriter in Greenbrae, Calif., mails clients and prospects **a free newsletter showcasing his ideas** for attention-getting campaigns. Levison pays just 75 cents to publish and mail each two-sided newsletter, sent to over 1,200 software marketing professionals every two months. He also encourages readers to forward the newsletter to associates, partners, or clients.

Levison's newsletter helps him build exposure, credibility, and business. The time and cost of publishing it is insignificant compared to the significant revenues it generates each year. Levison says, "The newsletter reminds my prospects of me every two months and has dramatically enhanced my image and credibility in the industry."

"Your most effective marketing tool may be your own customer list, but you'd better make sure you have one. A lot of people think they can just use the list of companies they send bills to. Wrong. That's a billing list. If you want a marketing list, you have to generate one, and that means including the information a marketer needs, which is a lot different from the information a credit manager needs."

ERNAN ROMAN
author of *Integrated Direct Marketing:
Techniques and Strategies for Success*
(McGraw-Hill, 1988)

55
IDEA

Free Catalog Offer

For the first 10 years of its existence, supermarkets wouldn't give Stash Tea, a 25-year-old company in Tigard, Ore., the time of day. Then it placed a small advertisement for its tea catalog on the back of its foil wrapper, which itself was designed in-house. Thousands of letters began pouring in. Now Stash has won two Gold Echo awards—the direct-marketing equivalent of the Oscars.

Their success started when they **offered a free catalog on their packaging**. "Basically, we developed this list of qualified leads at no cost to us," says Tom Lisicki, president of Stash Tea. "We were getting a 6% to 8% response rate just by sending the catalogs out." But then Stash went one better: Three years ago the company began including a personal note with each catalog. An on-line database of the letters and sophisticated querying capabilities made the task fairly easy. The response rate jumped to nearly 30%. Armed with a printout of people clamoring for its tea, Stash has pushed its way into retail stores around the country.

56
IDEA

Prescription for a Product

What's the best way to reach your customer? Armando Cuervo used none of the traditional marketing vehicles. Instead, he **catered to an audience that would recommend his products**.

Cuervo had invented a device for cribs that simulates car motion and sound, which stopped most colicky babies from crying during research tests. After a year of disappointing sales in baby stores, Cuervo began targeting an audience that would understand and appreciate his scientific research: pediatricians. So, he started attending pediatric conventions and sending direct mail to pediatricians.

The results were much better. Today his company, Sweet Dreams in Westerville, Ohio, sells its SleepTight Infant Soother only by phone, offering a 15-day free trial (800-NO-COLICK). Cuervo, who reports sales close to $500,000, says most of his referrals come from pediatricians.

Worth a Thousand Words

Enclosing a meaningful snapshot of your product with a sales letter is a cheap way to boost your direct mail response, as Robert Scheer, a Canadian-based video producer, discovered.

To sell his new video, "How to Raise a Happy, Healthy Chow Chow," Scheer sent a letter describing the product to all the Chow breeders he could find. **Along with the letter, he included a picture** of a champion Chow and his breeder grooming him, with a video camera in the foreground. The letter began, "I thought you would be interested in seeing this snapshot of 'Mikey' I took while making my new video."

The photo prints cost him about 30 cents each. "But it was worth it," said Scheer, whose letters pulled a whopping 14% response rate.

58
IDEA

Bagging the Customer

As the saying goes, "Do what you've always done and you'll get what you've always gotten." With traditional direct mail, that's usually a 1% to 2% response rate, because most envelopes don't even get opened. To stand out in a mailbox, consider "pushing the envelope."

John Cooper, a professional speaker and trainer, was targeting human resource departments in major corporations with a message about his luncheon program, "Humor in the Workplace." Instead of envelopes, he sent his mail in brown paper bags. The outside of the bags was stamped in bold letters, "A Great Speaker Is in the Bag!"

Did it work? "You bet it did," says Cooper. The campaign netted a 10% response. Even those who didn't book his program said it was innovative, outrageous, and funny, which helped support Cooper's identity as "America's Creative Communicator."

With a repeat mailing, you might send a different type of envelope each time, to break through the mailbox clutter. One manufacturer sent out three separate mailings: one in a neon bubble-type envelope, the next in a firecracker-red mailing tube, and lastly a plastic water sipper with the address label imprinted directly on the product. The response rate was a hefty 37%.

59

IDEA

Ride-Along Mail

Jeff Edelman, founder of start-up catalog house SoHo Designs in Dobbs Ferry, N.Y., needed less costly and more effective ways to introduce teenagers to his collection of artsy T-shirts and hats. A mailing broker told him of **private mail-delivery services**, such as Alternative Postal Delivery (616-235-2828), that could couple his catalog in a polybag with *Seventeen* magazine, which is geared to teen readers.

The drawback: the ride-along program extended to only a tiny fraction of *Seventeen*'s readership. The advantage: It's a great way to test the market. And it's cheaper than using the U.S. Postal Service. Edelman's mailing cost $60 per 1,000 catalogs using private delivery, compared to $200 by mail. Heartened by the response from *Seventeen* readers in several major cities, Edelman planned a bigger mailing, of 50,000 catalogs, using private postal delivery.

Fax on Demand

A system that provides customers with information at their convenience works around the clock for Dan Poynter, author of 75 books and founder of Para Publishing in Santa Barbara, Calif.

Customers interested in his books and reports call 805-968-8947 from their fax machines and choose from a menu of information on self-publishing, book promotion, fax-on-demand systems, skydiving, and other topics Poynter writes about. Each document includes information on how to order Para Publishing books and how to buy Poynter's 10-page reports via fax-on-demand.

Para Publishing's line receives over 100 calls a day, 24 hours a day. And because it's a one-step system, faxes are sent on the customer's dime. It even works for international customers.

"As a result of the system, **more than 60% of our orders now arrive electronically: by e-mail, fax, and telephone**," says Poynter. "Fax-on-demand relieves some of the workload while serving our customers. Now, we are making money while we sleep."

61

IDEA

Wire Mail

From a farmhouse in the cornfields of Spring Grove, Minn., Audio Computer Information cofounder John Stewart is trying a new attention grabber, the seemingly old-fashioned telegram, to market and sell ads on his weekly radio program about computers.

Within a tight budget, Stewart wanted to expand his broadcast reach, but first he had to attract attention from station managers and media buyers. Western Union (800-624-5472) offers DeskMail, a modemized link through which a message is typed on a PC and transmitted directly to Western Union, where it's formatted and dispatched as a telegram look-alike with the familiar Western Union label. Studies show an 86% open-and-read rate for these telegrams.

Stewart **fires off one-page "wires" through DeskMail** for a mere $3.90 each for overnight delivery. He considers it a bargain because "you don't use your own stationery, don't have to print the letters, and don't have to take them to the post office."

Once recipients peer inside the curiosity-inducing envelope, they're impressed. "It delivers the perception that you really mean business, because recipients assume you've gone to a lot of extra effort"—which, Stewart concedes, he hasn't. "Even if you're working out in the country on a single laptop," he concludes, "you come off looking like a major corporation from downtown."

62
IDEA

Seductive Sweepstakes

Murray Raphel developed Gordon's Alley into a multimillion-dollar pedestrian mall in Atlantic City, N.J. The reason for his success: direct mail. In his 30 years of marketing experience, he has used various tactics, but one of his most successful direct-mail promotions was literally a gamble: **announcing a sale with a sweepstakes**. Usually when Raphel mailed a "SALE" notice to customers, the average response was 5% to 8%. When he added a sweepstakes, the return jumped to 10% or 12%.

Running a sale with a sweepstakes and adding the customer's name on the entry form increases response an additional 5% to 10%. Originally, Raphel told customers to fill in their names and addresses, and bring the sweepstakes certificate to the store. Then he preprinted each customer's name on the entry form. Response jumped from around 10% to almost 18%.

Fax Broadcast

Within nine months of being fired from an executive position with a large national publishing company, Ernest Oriente had 64 clients paying him $300 to $500 per month by credit card for a weekly telephone call of 30 to 40 minutes. The key to his instant success, he maintains, was **fax broadcast technology**.

Each month he uses his Macintosh computer and Delrina WINfax software (Symantec, $150) to fax a monthly, one-page "success" article to 3,700 targeted publishing prospects and 180 business magazines. Articles such as "How can positively outrageous service increase your income?" and "Three easy ways to know your competition" have been featured in the *L.A. Times, Incentive Magazine,* Newstrack Executive Tapes, *Bottom Line* newsletter and *Electronic Retailer.* His home-based telephone consulting and coaching practice works with companies that compete directly with his former employer.

Oriente reports he faxes 24 hours a day for four days straight to reach almost 4,000 numbers. He explains, "I've programmed the order of my distribution so each long-distance call costs between 12 cents and 18 cents per fax. It's a lot cheaper than direct mail or relying on a sales force."

"Marketers have a unique promotional advantage when their proprietary databases function as private media. For example, they can generate additional sales by promoting product A to other members of their database who resemble known buyers of product A. Or they can cross-promote products C, D, and G to their product A buyers because they know and can exploit their buyers' product and sales 'hot buttons.' Because they have proprietary knowledge of consumers' individual characteristics, marketers can test-market new products with target segments before making a full market introduction."

JOCK BICKERT
National Demographics and Lifestyles, Denver, Colo.
The Direct Marketing Handbook
(McGraw-Hill, 2nd edition, 1992)

64
IDEA

P.S. Attention

Most people use a P.S. in their letter as an afterthought. But Ted Nicholas, author of *Magic Words That Bring You Riches* (813-596-4966), knows direct marketers who have seen response increase by 300% by **adding an effective P.S. to a sales letter**. And Siegfried Vogele, professor of direct marketing in Munich, Germany, has done extensive eye tests on what people look at in a mailing piece. First, they look to see who sent it, then at how the letter is addressed; then their eye jumps to the signature. The next thing they read is the P.S.

Nicholas suggests making it a practice to use a P.S. in every sales letter. His ideas for the most successful P.S. messages:

- Motivate the prospect to action.
- Reinforce the offer.
- Emphasize or introduce a bonus.
- Introduce a surprise benefit.
- Emphasize price or terms of your offer.
- Emphasize tax deductibility of purchase.
- Emphasize guarantees.

65
IDEA

Open Sesame

Recipients sort and prioritize their mail according to clues on the envelopes. So, how do you get your direct mail opened and read instead of tossed? Joan Throckmorton, president of a direct-marketing consulting firm in Pound Ridge, N.Y., offers some **clever ideas to make your envelopes more enticing**:

- Print a teaser on the envelope to get the reader inside, such as "Five Ways to Double Your Net Profit."
- Send a blind mailing—a plain envelope with a small return address that does not reveal the business name. Throckmorton says, "Blind mailings work because people feel they'd have to open it to find out what's inside."
- Personalize the mailing as much as possible, starting with the recipient's name. Try to avoid using "occupant" or titles like "Manager" or "CEO."
- Use a third-class pre-cancelled stamp, which carries a bulk rate but looks like a real 32 cent stamp, instead of a bulk-rate insignia. Real stamps suggest a more personal mailing.
- Send your mailings in closed-face envelopes (envelopes without windows). They are more likely to be opened than window envelopes, which are commonly used for bills.

66
IDEA

Going to the Top

Small companies often complain that it's difficult to reach decision makers in large corporations. But Stuart Herskovitz, founder of Qosina Corp. in Farmingdale, N.Y., penetrated the world's biggest cosmetics manufacturers and **cultivated a new market by mailing his information repeatedly to their CEOs**.

Herskovitz, who for 12 years had manufactured plastic parts such as clamps and connectors for the medical market, was walking through Macy's when he noticed one woman after another trying lipstick from the same tube. The health-conscious Herskovitz sensed a waiting market for disposable plastic items.

He went back to the office, stuffed envelopes with his catalog, price list, and assorted samples, and mailed them off to the CEOs of the country's largest cosmetics companies. Within a few weeks Herskovitz got a call from a vice-president of one of those companies. Converting those first qualified leads into sales, though, took about two years of solid correspondence. Herskovitz continued to send catalogs and more product samples to everyone on his prospect list, regardless of who responded to his initial mailing. To induce more cosmetics companies to give him a call, he began mailing the catalog to some 500 chain-store cosmetics-counter executives.

Six years after his walk through Macy's, Qosina's "Qosmedix" line of sponges, cotton swabs, and throwaway plastic applicators accounted for one-third of its total sales, which exceeded $3 million.

67

IDEA

Keep the Best, Trim the Rest

Many mail-order companies are lowering their postal costs by **cutting back their mailing list to their real or best customers**. Here's how some of them separate the browsers from the buyers.

The Sharper Image, a high-tech gadget catalog business in San Francisco, figures each duplicate name on its mailing list is worth at least 10 bucks. So, every person who calls the company to report receiving more than one catalog a month gets a $10 gift certificate. The company eliminates 1,000 to 1,500 duplicates a month that way. When you're mailing two million catalogs a month, it adds up.

Performance Bicycle of Chapel Hill, N.C., slapped a large red "Last Catalog" sticker on its holiday issue, warning recipients that if they wanted to continue receiving the catalog, they had to become customers. The abrupt-warning tactic has helped Performance weed out everyone but the serious bike shoppers, says Randy Martin, vice-president of marketing.

Fox Valley Spring Inc., a $3-million maker of industrial springs in Appleton, Wis., wanted to grease the wheels for its initial catalog mailing, so first it sent out a glossy postcard as an invitation to call for the catalog. The responses gave Fox Valley a targeted list for a more costly catalog mailing, plus its first set of customers. Three to five percent of those who received the postcard alone put in orders, and 6% of the postcard recipients called for the catalog.

Take Pen in Hand

Amidst the automation engendered by the electronic revolution, a little personal attention can go a long way. Baron C. Hanson, the "Head Buckaroo" of FlexCorp, a manufacturer of translucent plastic business cards in Charlotte, N.C., still writes personal notes by hand, and even has mass-mailing envelopes addressed by hand.

Upon buying a 5,000-name database of advertising specialty distributors and retail print shops, Hanson sent a **handwritten note** to each contact, along with samples of his cards and a price list. Although the mailing took three months to complete, FlexCorp's response was a whopping 46%. Sales of its printed-plastics line rose by 133% that year. And because the personalized mail was going out in small batches of 100 each day, it was easy for customer service to handle the steady flow of orders.

Enclose a Dream Ticket

We've all received direct mail promising unbelievable prizes, only to be disappointed when we open the envelope and there's a catch. However, one gamble that's on the up-and-up and needs no explaining is a state-run lottery.

Andy Juster and Scott Pilato, cofounders of Sunny Manufacturing, a $3-million waterbed manufacturer in Longwood, Fla. decided to **make good marketing use of their state lottery's credibility**. They stuffed lottery tickets into mailings they sent to the top 100 mattress retailers to announce a new line of bedroom furniture. The mailings specified when Sunny Waterbeds would follow up with a call. "Lottery ticket enclosed" was printed on the envelope.

The net result? When Sunny Waterbeds called a week later to announce the winning number, 70% of the prospects took the call and listened to its pitch. Usually only 15% take the follow-up call on a mailing. "We were surprised," says Juster. "You wouldn't expect these people, who are really important, to hold on to a $1 lottery ticket for a week."

70

IDEA

Prospect Releases

Leave it to a public-relations firm to teach other businesses how to stretch their own PR dollars. For many years, Floathe Johnson Associates (now Evans Group Technology in Seattle, Wash.) **sent news releases on its own progress directly to prospective clients**.

About once a month, an announcement of a new account, award won, or new hire went out to 100 members of the press, 150 clients, and 500-plus prospects. Under such circumstances, it can be tempting to turn a news release into a sales pitch. Resist the urge, counsels senior vice-president Chuck Pettis, or the release will alienate the press and won't impress prospects. "People said they read about us in the paper," adds Pettis. "Nine times out of 10, I'll bet they were remembering the press release."

One to five prospects per news release called to learn more, making it the top generator of new business leads for the firm.

71
IDEA

Catalogs on Video

Polymer Plastics Corp., a seller of circuit-board products, had found a way for its direct-mail campaign to bypass the circular file. "If customers got a videotape in the mail, I figured they were going to have to look at it," said CEO Larry Stock. "Curiosity alone was going to kill them."

It turned out that customers didn't just look, they responded. When **video catalogs** accompanied the paper catalogs, they generated 20 times the response of paper catalogs sent alone. After the videotapes were introduced, stagnant sales of one product line jumped from $10,000 to more than $20,000 a month. Sales of Polymer's products had tripled to $2.3 million in the two years since the Mountain View, Calif., company started sending out the video catalogs.

Stock's videos piqued the interest of both customers and distributors. Because the tapes demonstrated how to use the products, they also served as a sales and training tool that distributors could use when calling on customers.

Happy Birthday, Dear Customer

Instead of searching for new customers to keep your company growing, persuade those you have to buy more. Robert Sidell, owner of California Cosmetics in Chatsworth, Calif., thought if he could just **get his existing customers to spend another $10 a head**, he could grow his $12-million company by another $4 million. He discovered by accident just how easy it could be. More out of idle curiosity than anything else, he had his service reps call 10 customers who hadn't ordered in a while to find out why. Eight placed orders immediately. Clearly, customers liked to be remembered, and they returned the favor with new orders.

Since Sidell's order takers routinely asked the birth dates of the customers, he decided to send them birthday presents with his catalog. The gift was nothing fancy—a set of three small makeup brushes that cost 45 cents. The whole package, including postage, cost him $1. He didn't know whether they were grateful or felt guilty, but 40% of the people who got birthday presents immediately placed orders. That was a 40% repeat rate, compared with the 12% he had been averaging.

73
IDEA

Go Fish with Gifts

Companies of any size or interest can **reel in new customers by using inex-pensive gifts** to bait their direct-mail hook. The Economic Development Corporation of Utah (EDCU), a nonprofit organization that brings capital investment into the state, reached non-traditional business relocation advisors.

For a mailing with an authentic fish on its line to 3,000 lawyers, accountants, and investment bankers who influence capital decisions, EDCU embossed the front of its brochure with a replica of the Utah Priscacara, a fish indigenous to the state about 50 million years ago. The brochure read: "Utah Has Been Making Lasting Impressions for Eons...Now It's Your Turn to Be Impressed!" Recipients could return a tear-off reply card to receive a plaster casting of the Priscacara, perfect for use as a paperweight.

A 10% immediate response to the mailing and continuing requests for the EDCU's services made this a worthwhile fishing expedition. "The way we look at it," said Chris Roybal, EDCU's vice president for client services, "that fossil reminds corporate decision-makers to consider Utah for expansion and relocation opportunities."

74
IDEA

Letter Perfect

Little touches can make a big difference in your mail return. After 20 years of trial and error experience, Susanna K. Hutcheson—an advertising and direct-mail copywriter and consultant (http://www.powerwriting. com) in Wichita, Kans.—knows **what it takes to get a big mail pull from a direct-mail campaign**. Here are some of her secrets:

- End a page of your sales letter with an incomplete sentence. It makes the reader want to turn to the next page.
- Use lots of subheads. If the subheads interest readers enough, they will draw them in to the letter.
- Use short testimonials. People love to see what others say about you. Just a few sentences and their names and locations will do.
- Put extra enticements in handwriting. Use the same color ink you sign the letter with. Make it look as if you've added some benefits at the last minute.
- Write a message on the envelope. Seven out of 10 recipients open the envelope if there is a handwritten message on the outside.

Salvage from a Spreadsheet

For years, AAA Small Auto World, a salvaged-parts dealer in Fort Worth, Tex., added names to its database until it had 350,000 garages and body shops in the United States on file. CEO Ron Sturgeon kept inflating the advertising budget to keep pace with his growing database, but even with in-house production, a single comprehensive mailing would cost a whopping $100,000.

Sturgeon turned to his computer to narrow his focus and make his mailings a lot more profitable. Sturgeon created a **sortable spreadsheet that tracked vital statistics**: sales performance by state, type of customer, amount of sale, and ad or direct-mail piece.

If his monthly report told him, for example, that 60 phone queries from Utah yielded only one sale, he diverted marketing money to states with a closing rate of better than 60 to one. Eventually, retail outlets in high-response states made up about half of Sturgeon's mailing list, so concentrating his marketing money on those areas substantially improved sales.

By tracking ad responses, monitoring phone-call-to-sale ratios, and staggering mailings, the company trimmed 40% from its marketing budget, sales grew 10% a year, and profits held steady in a beleaguered industry. Sturgeon said, "If you can't measure your marketing, you have to question if it's worth doing."

Monkeying with the Mail

The post office will send just about anything you can put a stamp on. So, to **attract hard-to-reach prospects**, Claudia Cannon, director of marketing for Booklines Hawaii, sends them coconuts.

Cannon collects the coconut shells that fall from the trees in her backyard for use as a marketing weapon. When she encounters a prospect who doesn't return her calls, she writes a short message on the outside of the nut, stamps $3 on it, and sends it out priority mail.

She only sends out about 30 coconuts a year, but 90% of those who receive the ovoid "postcard" call her immediately when the nut reaches their desks. In one instance, Cannon had spent more than three months trying to get the buyer for the Navy Exchange store to call her back. As soon as he received the coconut, he called immediately, and Booklines ended up with an additional $100,000 in annual sales from the Navy Exchange store.

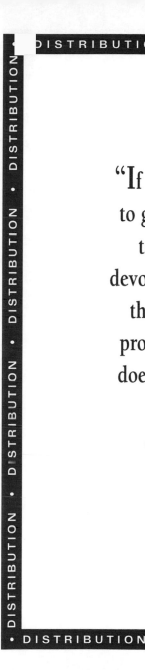

V

"If a product isn't selling, I want to get it out of there because it's taking up space that can be devoted to another part of my line that moves. Besides, having a product languish on the shelves doesn't do much for our image."

NORMAN MELNICK
chairman of Pentech International, Edison, N.J.

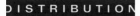

77

IDEA

Rev Up Your Retailers

Oil the gears of your distribution machine by **sending your resellers a newsletter to help sell your products**. Creativity for Kids, an 80-person toy manufacturer, sent a newsletter—called *Fingerprint*—to retailers in 4,000 business locations three times a year. It routinely showcased innovative customer practices and passed on hints to boost sales.

One article explained how to orchestrate an in-store sales event in which retailers could run hands-on activities for parents and children. The story inspired 600 stores to order discounted promotional learning kits. The newsletter also included interviews with child-development experts, to help retailers understand the value of the toys they were selling, and contests to encourage interaction with customers, draw attention to new products, and track readership. One such event was the annual challenge, which asked readers to predict which would be the best-selling new Creativity for Kids product.

"The newsletter was enormously popular with our customers, who used it to help run their businesses," said Phyllis Brody, co-owner of Creativity for Kids. And it also helped to enhance the relationship between manufacturer and retailer.

78

IDEA

Surrogate Distribution

If you have the right product, licensing your product or technology may be an attractive alternative to traditional distribution. Rick Chitty, CEO of IQ Software in Norcross, Ga., built his software company around the idea of getting somebody else to deal with the hassles of distribution.

Chitty and his partners licensed their report-writing software to other software developers who were writing for a variety of specialized industries. Chitty's theory: whether the software was for accountants or pharmacists, the end-users would want a variety of options for printing out their data. It would be cheaper and easier for software publishers to license IQ's software than to write their own.

IQ Software receives an up-front licensing fee as well as royalties. Chitty says his company now licenses its software to some 700 clients, who sell it under some 500 to 600 different names. Although licensing means giving up much of the profit, it's worth it to Chitty, who claims that his $8-million company has grown an average of 90% a year, with pretax margins in excess of 20%. "I'm interested in literally sitting in the background and clipping my little royalty coupons," he says.

79
IDEA

Home Shopping Spree

Retail distribution slowed our growth," states Brenda French, owner of French Rags in Los Angeles. "Buyers had no idea what their customers wanted, and retailers weren't merchandising effectively. We were making clothes for retailers, not customers." French's solution? She **created her own distribution network by selling through consultants** at their homes.

Several years ago, a customer offered to show French Rags designer knitwear to friends. The customer set up one-hour, one-on-one appointments with her new clients, offering fashion advice and letting them try things on. The clothes would be made to order and delivered within six weeks. Almost everyone who came to a consultation ordered clothing.

Today, French is completely out of retail. She sends a new line of clothing to her 120 trained consultants every three to four months. "If retail sales equal x, direct sales turned out to be $10x$," proclaims French. "And since everything is made to order, we don't have to guess. We have greater profitability because there is no inventory and no returns."

80
IDEA

Pushcart Your Way Upward

Selling your products on mall pushcarts and kiosks can bring in $55,000 in a holiday season, and it's a low-risk way to test the retail market.

United Vision Group made its way to success by stepping rung by rung up the retail ladder. This manufacturer of handsome wooden gifts, based in Ossining, N.Y., is one of a few *Inc.* 500 companies that have **moved their products on pushcarts**. "It's hectic when you open November 1 and close December 31," admits Joseph Coyne, former vice-president of sales at United Vision. But the ruthless selling cycle taught the company invaluable lessons about product mix and product life cycles.

After a while, several mall developers asked United Vision to take over vacant stores for a season. The pushcart sales indicated sites ripe for expansion, and United Vision opened its first permanent store, called PG Arbor, in New Jersey's Rockaway Town Square Mall. Meanwhile, the company's 200-odd carts and kiosks, in malls from Seattle to South Florida, have kicked in 60% of its annual sales.

81
IDE

What a Good Name Can Do

Even if you don't have an established brand, you can **license a well-known brand name and put it on your product** to get into retail stores.

Licensed merchandise has exploded in the marketplace in recent years, and the trend isn't limited to lunch boxes. Of course, it's an investment. You can expect to pay from 5% to 12% of wholesale revenues to the licenser over the life of the agreement, in addition to up-front costs.

Opus, a bird-feeder maker in Bellingham, Mass., negotiated a license with Disney because John Stone, president of the second-generation family business, wanted to tap the burgeoning kids' market. Stone invested $50,000 in product design, merchandising, and promotion. He worked with Disney through the year-long design and development process. The payoff? The Disney name helped to place Opus products in about 3,000 stores.

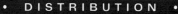

82
IDEA

Trade Margin for National Ads

Companies often expect their independent dealers to shoulder the job of creating new-product demand. CyCare, a software publishing unit of HBO & Co., in Scottsdale, Ariz., avoided problems by **asking its dealers what they wanted** from CyCare before introducing Physician Practice Director, a software program used to manage small medical practices. The 160 dealers asked CyCare to promote its products with a national ad campaign, and they were willing to help pay for it by giving up some margin.

Cycare tested potential ads on doctors and surveyed two years' worth of magazines before selecting nine journals in which to buy space. The ads included an 800 number to call for a free video.

All leads from the national ads were passed on to the dealers. In two years, Cycare sold over 1,500 units. Director Jerry Hyman said, "It's generally too expensive to create leads from national advertising, but since dealers were flexible on pricing, we were both able to benefit from this campaign."

83

IDEA

Souped-Up Demo

Go shopping for shirts and walk out with lentils—well, why not? In its start-up days, Buckeye Beans & Herbs conducted a daring demo of its dry-bean soups at an upscale retail store in Walnut Creek, Calif. "We handed out samples as people walked in," recalls Jill Smith, founder of the company. "We sold out of product that day."

So, did Buckeye go on to crack major supermarkets nationwide? Guess again. Big grocers charge "slotting fees," which can cut into a marketer's profits. Instead, Buckeye **used the retail exposure to gain entry to small specialty shops**. Being in a high-class department store gave it credibility as a company and as a product category. Says co-owner Doug Smith, "We made sure our brokers knew about it; they'd tell distributors, who'd tell retailers."

The demonstration—conceived at a trade show—opened many doors. Fourteen years later, more than 6,000 specialty stores carry the soups, giving Buckeye 1996 revenues of $7 million.

84

IDEA

Product Becomes Service

To first-time entrepreneurs, it may seem easier to sell a commodity than to build a long-term relationship with a new client. But service customers want their questions answered by a real person.

Tyler Phillips, founder of the Partnership Group, a pioneer in child-care and elder-care referral services in Lansdale, Pa., wanted to market his services by selling informational kits to employees through the human resource departments of large companies. The kits, which spelled out a range of his company's services, opened doors into a company, but the employees weren't buying them. Phillips' strategy wasn't building rapport with the employees, who were his "real" customers.

Phillips stopped trying to sell to employees and **began offering companies a consulting service for all employees**. He also changed from per-kit pricing to an annual fee that covers a client's total workforce. His contracts gave workers unlimited access to the Partnership Group and helped to create new options for their children's care. Ten years after abandoning the kits, Phillips had sold 109 three-year contracts and 20 open-ended deals.

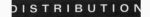

REAL
WORLD

"Quality, quality, quality: never waver from it, even when you don't see how you can afford to keep it up. When you compromise, you become a commodity and then you die. And besides, the problem with the rat race is that when you win, you are still a rat."

GARY HIRSHBERG
founder of Stonyfield Farm Yogurt,
Wilton, N.H.

Playing with the Big Boys

Today, mass merchandisers book about 40% of all U.S. retail sales, and none casts a longer shadow than the discount retailer. To win the hearts of superstore buyers, take advice from John Koss, Jr., sales vice-president of an audio product manufacturer in Milwaukee, Wis., that makes well over 75% of its income from electronics superstores and discount department stores. Koss must be doing something right. His company recently surpassed $36 million in annual sales.

Here are Koss's **keys to getting in the door of megastores**:

- *Offer a great product priced to move rapidly.* The Koss product line, once reserved for audio aficionados, has expanded to cover a wide range of price points and products, including PC accessories.
- *Use catchy packaging.* Koss is always trying to improve the company's point-of-sale displays.
- *Update your office systems.* Wal-Mart, Target, and other large chains don't write paper orders any more. Koss has had electronic data interchange (EDI) in place since 1993.
- *Deliver.* It's not unusual for power retailers to expect turnaround in three to five days. And, Koss says, "You can't ship Wal Mart short, or it cancels the order."
- *Hit the pavement.* Sales reps are important to certain chains while others, like Wal-Mart, all but ban them. Those chains want to talk directly with company owners.

86
IDEA

Fundraising Channel

Jazz It Up had success selling its detachable sequin appliqués at fundraisers, grossing as much as $40,000 at a good show. The Nutcracker Market, where such events are held, collects $500 and up for space, plus 10% of sales.

Keven Wilder, owner of a Chicago-based retail/catalog business of upscale home accessories, toys, and desk items, added the names of 25,000 qualified leads to her mailing list through her travels to fundraiser shows around the country. She opened a Chiasso store in Los Angeles after a profitable exhibit at the Christmas Co., an Orange County Junior League event that draws 20,000 to Newport Beach, Calif.

Also popular are the Junior League holiday marts in Austin, Denver, and Washington, D.C. It's not exactly easy—most shows are held during the busiest selling season. Still, Wilder considers them **a good way "to test-market, advertise, and get names** without spending a lot."

87

IDEA

Big Company Piggyback

How did two entrepreneurs get their product offer on the shelves of every supermarket in the nation? By negotiating a comarketing arrangement with a large company that had wide distribution.

Leslie Lawrence and Nancy Urbschat ran a small ad agency and got into the new-products business when Lawrence became pregnant. "I wanted to keep a journal during my pregnancy," she says, but not finding anything she liked, the partners created a 40-week undated calendar they christened "Mother in the Making."

The duo decided that the product "wouldn't do well sitting in a bookstore." Instead, they figured they'd try to **get a big company to help them market it as a product tie-in**. Their target: Warner-Lambert, maker of e.p.t., a home-pregnancy test. Their goal was to get a calendar offer tucked into each e.p.t. box. But first they had to get a meeting with e.p.t.'s product manager, and that took a good six months.

When Lawrence and Urbschat showed up, they were prepared. They arrived at the meeting with a marketing strategy in hand, which distinguished their idea from the other pregnancy-related product ideas the manager had seen. Five months later, they had a contract: the East Longmeadow, Mass., entrepreneurs and their company, The Super Market, would print the coupons and calendars at their own expense, and Warner-Lambert would receive $1 per sale. A year later, the offer hit the shelves. Orders were sluggish, but the exposure was worth it: a vitamin company and a hospital called, both requesting deals to use the calendars as premiums.

Together We Sell

Fighting for shelf space? Here's a solution: **form a cooperative group with competitors to persuade retailers to carry all your products**.

That strategy worked for Tony Pereira, president of Clear and Simple, in West Simsbury, Conn. His software publishing company makes applications for a small segment of the computer market that uses IBM's OS/2 computer operating system. Instead of fighting the battle for shelf space alone, Pereira brought together over two dozen other developers and formed the OS/2 Vendor Council to encourage retailers to carry their software.

The vendors cooperated by creating brochures with all members' products, and launched a joint advertising campaign in national magazines. Together, the group developed a merchandising program with flyers and in-store displays. They offered to add the retailers' names to national ads, and even convinced IBM to help fund the advertising. "This effort has gotten us onto store shelves and has generated new sales for me," says Pereira.

89
IDEA

Milking Customer Loyalty

To establish contact with its customers, Stonyfield Farm stamps "Let us hear from you" on the back of its yogurt cartons. Stonyfield also communicates to its fans through its newsletter, *Moos from the Farm,* where it introduces new products and promotions. By **encouraging fans to spread the word about its products**, the New Hampshire maker of "farm style" yogurt was able to get into supermarkets and compete with much bigger companies.

In the early 1990s, Stonyfield announced an "Adopt-a-Cow" program, which encouraged frequent purchases and educated young customers about where the company gets its milk. Consumers who bought five cartons of Stonyfield Farm Yogurt, or 10 servings of its newest frozen yogurt, received a free photo and biography of a cow that produced milk for the company, an adoption certificate, plus a free subscription to the newsletter. Demand far exceeded the number of cows, so many consumers shared their adoptees.

The result of the program was increased sales—but more importantly, the company received publicity from area newspapers and magazines. The press coverage helped Stonyfield get exclusive frozen yogurt accounts, such as the University of Connecticut and Au Bon Pain, a French bakery with more than 120 shops nationwide at the time. The bottom line? "Word-of-mouth builds better loyalty than advertising," says Samuel Kaymen, chairman of Stonyfield Farm.

90
IDEA

Off-Season Incentives

If you suffer from a short selling season, talk to Alan Trusler, president of Aladdin Steel Products Inc., an $18-million manufacturer of wood-, gas-, and pellet-burning stoves in Colville, Wash. Until recently, the company's sales peaked with the fall foliage and petered out with winter's last snowstorms. Undaunted, Trusler **doubled his sales season** by using three strategies:

- *Early-bird incentives.* Trusler entices his 500 dealers to sell stoves in the middle of barbecue season by offering them steeper discounts for the entire year if they stock stoves in the off-peak months, March through July.
- *Flexible financing.* Floor-plan financing gets dealers products as needed. Dealers pay (with interest) a third-party finance company for units as they're sold. The finance company pays Aladdin up front. Trusler absorbs his dealers' interest expenses if they sell their units within eight months.
- *Cash discounts.* Dealers who pay for products up front get cash discounts for buying early: 8% off each invoice in March, 7% in April, 6% in May, and so on.

Trusler's strategies have helped even out cash flow, and Aladdin's production process can now run year-round, lowering manufacturing costs. Even with the aggressive discounts, Aladdin's pretax profits are twice the industry standard, and the company grew 247% between 1991 and 1996.

91
IDEA

Team Up with Megastore Buyers

Cap Toys in Bedford Heights, Ohio, has the same problem most manufacturers do: **How do you get on the shelf of the largest retailer in your industry**? For toy makers, that means Toys "R" Us. The giant retailer has up to 50 times as much space for toys as other toy sellers do, and smaller merchants watch closely what their big competitor buys. Trouble is, not much of that extensive shelving is up for grabs.

To get on the shelves of Toys "R" Us, John Osher, founder and president of Cap Toys, works closely with the megastore buyers to give them what they want. Osher shows them concepts of toys he's considering manufacturing. They develop packaging themes together and discuss pricing. If they don't want it, he doesn't argue—and doesn't make the toy. Finally, he makes sure the toy can sell itself on the shelf, since TV advertising is both costly and risky.

Once you're on the shelves, you have a good chance of staying there. Osher hopes for three to five years of sales from each toy, and he develops lines of toys that build on previous bestsellers. That's why Cap's revenues are up 2,392% since 1987. Osher reached his start-up goal—a $100-million company—last year.

92
IDEA

We Can Show It to You Wholesale

How does a small company **expand from local to national markets**? For Burt's Bees, in Raleigh, N.C., the answer was exhibiting at wholesale shows and selling to distributors.

In the sparsely populated reaches of central Maine, founders Roxanne Quimby and Burt Shavitz bottled honey in kitchen canning jars, cast candles out of beeswax on a wood stove, threw the finished lot into a pickup truck, and drove off to seasonal crafts fairs. After two years it struck Quimby that being on the road every weekend, coming back and making candles, then going on the road again was ridiculous. Plus, the team's market was limited to the territory they and their tiring Datsun could span.

They plowed their meager profits into an indoor space at a wholesale show and sat there and wrote orders. That, Quimby says, is when the business took flight. "We concentrated totally on wholesale," she says, "because it was easier to open markets that way than by retail." The company now sells more than 100 gift and skin-care products and has launched a line of country clothing.

93

IDEA

Old Product, New Players

How do you make a thousand-year-old idea new? **Repackage it, then launch it into new markets**. That's what Rex Games Inc., in San Francisco, has done with Tangoes™, its modern version of an ancient Chinese tangram game. President and CEO Mark Chester sells it as therapy, a training tool, an educational aid, and a sales premium, but rarely as just a game.

Less creative marketers might have forced the product into an obvious niche in the toy-and-game market. But then they might not be looking at nearly $2 million in sales, with precious little advertising. Chester and his partner cleverly positioned the product as a tool to spark creative thinking in the corporate-training market, improve problem solving in the educational market, speed recovery in the rehabilitation market, and allay trip boredom in the travel market.

Rex boasts customers ranging from New York City's Museum of Modern Art shop to American Express and Colgate-Palmolive. And the markets keep cross-fertilizing, Chester reports. "It may be an old game, but with so many possible uses, it has a long life ahead of it."

94
IDEA

Sampling with Elan

Product sampling—whether in a retail store, at a trade show, or at some other gathering of potential buyers—is low-tech, cheap, and cost-effective. It's especially useful for small companies that don't have the dollars big companies use to introduce new products.

Food companies, for instance, pay a demonstration company about $100 a day to supply a demonstrator and card table for a six-hour sampling shift. Most supermarket demos take place between 11 a.m. and 5 p.m., and your product will get into the hands or mouths of about 500 people. That's about 20 cents per person. Add the cost of the product consumed, the redemption cost of the coupons distributed, and the cost of training the demonstrators, to bring the total average cost up to about 30 cents per sample. Even mailing samples, which lacks the personal touch, costs more.

Joanne Biltekoff, who cofounded Elan, a frozen-yogurt maker in Buffalo, N.Y., lacked the capital for advertising blitzes and direct mail. Nonetheless, her company built up Elan to become the leading premium brand in some regions, primarily by using in-store demonstrations to get people to try it.

Elan graduated to a more balanced marketing strategy and expanded sales to more than 20 states. Even so, Elan used TV and print ads primarily to support the sampling program, which remained its flagship marketing medium.

95
IDEA

Preselling—All Viewers Great and Small

Disney and other corporate giants can create demand with money. Small businesses like The Lyons Group—a Dallas-based company—had to do it with smarts.

Sheryl Leach of The Lyons Group created Barney, the ubiquitous purple dinosaur who cavorts with a pack of real kids in a half-hour song-filled video aimed at preschool children. After a failure on the shelves of Toys "R" Us test markets, Leach realized she had to **create demand all the way down the distribution chain, both retail and wholesale**.

To get retail stores to stock the tapes, Leach had to presell consumers—kids and their parents. Leach sent free Barney videos to day-care centers in selected areas. Once the centers showed the tapes, the kids were hooked. At the same time, Leach used part-time telemarketers to tell area retailers what she was up to. When several had agreed to stock a few tapes, she sent the preschools a list of places where Barney was sold locally. Kids would nag parents, who would buy, and so the demand began.

Then Leach told retailers they could get Barney from their regular distributors if they'd help her persuade those distributors to buy from her. Retailers did—with letters, calls, and orders for Barney tapes. Demand was the best sales argument Leach could bring to the wholesalers.

Today, Barney tapes are sold in practically every major video outlet, as well as toy stores, catalogs, supermarkets, drugstores, and bookstores.

96
IDEA

Less Can Be More

Making a huge sale is great. But joy turns to regret if your customer gets stuck with merchandise and never orders again. "We don't believe in onetime deals," said Emery Klein, CEO of Alaron, an electronics importer and custom product designer. The Auburn Hills, Mich., company **encouraged customers to order less** so their cash wouldn't be locked up in inventory.

"We advised them to buy conservatively, and if the promotion went well, we told them we'd be here for them," said Klein. When stores ran low on an item, they could depend on Alaron to meet their needs, with delivery in about 10 days. Klein looked like a hero if customers sold out rather than overbought. Alaron sold more in the long run using this strategy.

97
IDEA

Give Your Distributor a Hand

If you have only one product in a distributor's catalog, make sure it gets the attention it deserves—**supplement your dealer-distributor network with your own salespeople**. Delta Technology International, a software business in Eau Claire, Wis., added four of its own salespeople to its distribution channel for the company's software package. They laid the groundwork for a sale, then turned over the closing and commissions to Delta's local distributor.

Selling to Delta's customers took an average of two to four months, and distributors didn't want to invest that amount of time, explained CEO Jim Anthony. But when his distributors made a little easy money thanks to the supplemental sales effort, it reminded them that the product did sell.

One closing can pay a salesperson's annual base salary, said Anthony. Thanks to this system, Delta's product moved onto the industry's top 20 bestseller list, and Anthony was able to hire another corporate salesperson.

98
IDEA

Upstairs, Downstairs

For a hot product to stay hot, it takes more than luck. For EPI—the Santa Monica, Calif., company that had the U.S. distribution rights to Epilady, a women's hair-removal device—the answer was **dual positioning, pricing, and distribution**.

Within six months of introducing Epilady into such high-end department stores as Bloomingdale's and Marshall Field, Sharon Krok-Feuer, vice-president of EPI Products, knew she had one of the hottest products to hit the U.S. personal-care market in years. But Remington was launching a similar product that could shut Epilady out of the mass market. To figure out how to get into mass-market outlets without alienating its upscale base, EPI introduced a deluxe model, packaged with accessories, into the high-end stores at a premium price. After six months, the company sharply discounted the original Epilady and sold them in mass-market stores.

"Some of the [high-end] department stores were a little upset at first," conceded Krok-Feuer, but the new unit sold well enough to alleviate their concerns. Besides, noted president and sister Arlene Krok, EPI soon brought out new products that "made a hell of a lot of money for the department stores." The Krok sisters' company didn't do so badly either. Sales hit $100 million that year and nearly tripled the following year.

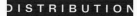

99
IDEA

Dare to Go Direct

Henry Kloss, cofounder and CEO of Cambridge SoundWorks in Newton, Mass., got consumers to shell out $500 for speakers, sight unseen and sound unheard. The trick? **Sell direct through advertising**. This tactic let Cambridge SoundWorks price the speakers hundreds of dollars below the competition, and made Kloss a figure as popular to stereo buffs as Santa Claus is to children.

The ad combination of Kloss and price was enough to get many audiophiles to dial the 800 number and talk to a salesperson. Overnight delivery took care of the rest. Even with the trial period, the return rate was less than 10%.

The strategy proved highly efficient. Because customers paid the company directly, Cambridge SoundWorks got its money at once. It needed no receivables financing, no credit department, no field sales force, and it didn't have to woo dealers at trade shows. "We could spend that money on advertising, paying our office salespeople well and putting more into the product," said Kloss. The company reached sales of $4 million in its first 12 months.

Look on the Label

When Elizabeth Andrews, CEO of The Baby Bag Co. in Cumberland, Maine, began selling her innovative infant outerwear, she made sure buyers could find her—even if they couldn't find a store that carried her goods. **She stitched her new company's address and phone number right onto every Baby Bag's label**.

Though Baby Bag had difficulty winning shelf space from retailers, potential customers who saw the products on the street were often intrigued enough to ask about them. Once they had the number, they could call Andrews to place an order or learn where the company's items were available for sale.

Later, when Baby Bag became better known, retailers objected to having the number on the label because they thought it would take business away from them. So, Andrews changed the tag to reveal the company's address but not its phone number. She still got plenty of calls from customers in rural regions who were serious enough to dial Directory Assistance to get the number. And the 800 retailers loved it because they got referrals.

101
IDEA

The Word is Out

One cold call to a dealer can start **word-of-mouth advertising** and get your product into stores.

Lynn Gordon, proprietor of French Meadow Bakery in Minneapolis, started her bread-making business in her kitchen, producing forty loaves a week for local co-ops. One day she made a cold call to a local gourmet shop, which started a word-of-mouth snowball. As luck would have it, the buyer was on a special diet, and Gordon's bread was just what she was looking for. Soon other grocery stores signed up. Meanwhile, customers sent loaves to friends around the country, who called to order more.

Under pressure from stores, distributors started asking for French Meadow bread. Next, Diane Sawyer and the *60 Minutes* crew showed up to do a story about the Women's Economic Development Corp., a program for women entrepreneurs in which Gordon was involved. Sawyer high-lighted Gordon and her gourmet bread on the show. Then the state helped subsidize a trip to the International Fancy Food & Confection Show in Chicago, where 300 stores placed orders. Will Steger, the tundra explorer, ordered Gordon's bread for the international trip he was leading across the Antarctic. Even Neiman Marcus bought French Meadow bread to include in a $5,000 Ultimate Cocktail Buffet.

As a result of that first cold call, Gordon moved her operation into a 13,500-square-foot storefront bakery in Minneapolis, where she eventually employed 15 people.

102
IDEA

Piggyback Storefront

Looking for customers? Why not set up shop within another store? When you **partner with an existing storefront**, your overhead is virtually nonexistent. Usually, a store-within-a-store pays a percentage of its revenues to its host in exchange for taking up what is most often less than 100 square feet of space. You have no lease to worry about and no utilities or fixed operating costs to pay. To hear the piggybackers tell it, it's the only way to sell.

Larry Margolis offered car phones from inside automobile dealerships and at car washes. "The piggyback idea works," said Margolis, who started the Car Phone Connection in Parsippany, N.J., in 1995. "Our start-up costs were next to nothing."

But the biggest advantage from Margolis's point of view was that his stores were instantly profitable. If a store sold four or five phones a week it was doing fine. He didn't have a huge overhead to meet. On average he paid the host, such as the automobile dealer, $75 to $100 per unit. So, if he didn't sell a lot of phones, his rent remained low.

Even Distributors Like Getting Samples

Dealers, sales representatives, and distributors are much more likely to sell a product they can show the customer. One way to encourage them to show your product is to make sure they have a **sample or demonstration version**.

Jayline International Group in Elizabeth, N.J., manufactures promotional items, such as pens, cups, and balls with company names imprinted on them. Its distribution involves drop-shipping orders directly to customers on behalf of one of 15,000 promotional and specialty product distributors across the country.

Once Jayline has shipped an order of imprinted water bottles to the distributor's customer, owner Jay Weinstock sends some overrun samples to the distributor. That's not common practice in the industry—most distributors never see what's sent to the customer. But Weinstock does it for many of his distributors because it helps stimulate sales.

Often distributors display the samples in their showroom or photograph them for their catalog. It makes it easy for distributors to sell that product to other clients. So when a customer asks for the same product, the distributor naturally orders from Jayline instead of from competitors. According to Weinstock's data, Jayline's strategy has helped increase business 25% from the distributors who have received samples.

104
IDEA

Help Your Products Sell Each Other

Can a **companion product boost your main product sales**? It did for Pleasant Rowland, president and founder of Pleasant Company, a mail-order operation in Middleton, Wis.

Rowland designed her American Girls Doll Collection to teach young girls about American history and give them a sense of self-awareness. Her catalog had an educational tone, teaching snippets of history while enticing girls and their mothers to buy the dolls. Rowland thought that kids would care more about the dolls if they became acquainted with the characters, so she had a collection of six books written to portray the dolls' lives and experiences.

In her Pleasant Company catalog, the dolls were packaged with the books. But outside her catalog, Rowland sold the books alone to stores and libraries. Each book contained a postage-paid reply card offering a free catalog, so book sales fed doll sales, and vice versa.

The companion books both enhanced the main product and generated money. In her first ten years, Rowland sold more than 40 million books and nearly four million dolls.

105
IDEA

They've Gotta Have It

Like candy in the checkout aisle, **place your merchandise prudently** and it will fly off the shelves.

Cane & Able's Robert Milgroom and his partner, Kevin Roseff, took existing elder-care products—like canes, magnifying lenses, and heat packs—that were not merchandised at all, and gave them a cohesive retail format. Milgroom saw a huge market in catering to the fastest-growing segment of the population, the over-75 set. So the pair developed eight-foot-wide, one-stop-shopping displays that more than 1,000 stores nationwide test-marketed. The strategy worked. Revenues for the new company, based in Edison, N.J., hit $35 million in just two years.

106
IDEA

If You Buy, You Will Sell

When launching a new product, arm yourself with the facts before your distributor asks, "Who's going to buy this from me?"

That's the question Ken Vaughan, president and CEO of Neoterik Health Technologies, an industrial safety-equipment manufacturer in Woodsboro, Md., kept hearing from distributors when he tried to sell them a new product. Now, Vaughan has the answer ready before he makes his sales pitch.

Vaughan and his sales team **poll 10 of each distributor's prospective customers** directly as to whether they'd buy Neoterik's products. Even if only half of them say yes, Neoterik uses this feedback to his advantage. "If the distributor doesn't buy our products," Vaughan said, "that's five customers they will lose to the competition."

Vaughan reported that his $10-million company has saved time and money with this sales strategy. With the traditional approach, it would take three to six visits—and many months—to convince distributors to carry his products. Now they make buying decisions almost immediately because the surveyed customers ask for the products.

VI

"Perhaps more than in any other situation, an international entrepreneur must be ready to forgo short-term profits in entering the multinational marketplace. It is imperative that your domestic operation be of such size and stability as to allow for generous test funds and a deferral of profits for a longer period of time than you might generally be accustomed to. It is also ill-advised to look at the foreign marketplace as a panacea for domestic problems. An organization that is strong and stable and is ready to commit time, money, and patience will be more apt to reap rewards than the quick-hitting opportunist."

RICHARD MILLER
Market Response International, North Chatham, Mass.
The Direct Marketing Handbook
(McGraw-Hill, 2nd edition, 1992)

107
IDEA

Foreign Intrigue

How did Husco Engineering, a small manufacturer in Connecticut, find international customers like Audi, Honda, Volkswagen, and Volvo? Richard Husta's company, which manufactures after-market automobile armrests, broke into foreign markets by **placing small, consistent ads in international trade magazines and commerce books**.

Husta found international advertising opportunities by asking the U.S. Department of Commerce, his suppliers, and salespeople from domestic trade magazines. He ran small advertisements that displayed his 800 number and Web page address in international car magazines, automobile industry trade magazines, and international trade books published by the federal government.

Husco averages 300 calls per month and handles steady hits to his Web page. Twenty-five percent of the calls turn into direct sales. Recently, his international exposure helped close contracts with Porsche, Saab, Toyota, and Isuzu.

103
IDEA

Rep Round Table

Restek, a manufacturer of lab-equipment parts, realized out of sight was out of mind for its foreign representatives from 30 countries. The solution: **gather the far-flung reps for three days of training at company headquarters** in Bellefonte, Pa.

Restek needed to know how to sell into secondary markets, so they prepared a grid that matched market niches with applications for its lab parts. The company intensified hands-on product training, and some reps even presented marketing mini-tutorials. Restek also paid attention to the reps' small but important requests: "Don't forget to forward us your press releases." "Don't send 'free' demo packages, because customs will assign them a value." "Please mail or fax product alerts as soon as there's a problem."

The company's portion of the bill (hotel and recreation included) came to about $50,000. Although it would have been cheaper to time a training session to a major trade show in Europe, the event on home turf allowed the reps to meet the whole Restek organization. "We reached some common ground," says Christine Vargo, who oversees the company's Western European operation. Before the gathering, 10% of Restek's $10.3 million in sales came from overseas. Within a year, that share grew to 25%.

109
IDEA

Hunting for Big Game Abroad

Trying to track down foreign companies willing to do business with you? Here are suggestions on where to get **international leads**:

- Call the Export Opportunity Hotline (800-243-7232) or the Trade Information Center (800-872-8723). Both are user-friendly services that can direct you to the sources that will best fulfill your lead-generation needs.
- Read Roger Axtell's *Do's and Taboos Around the World* (John Wiley & Sons, 1993, $14.95) as a desk reference. Regina Tracy, executive director of the Small Business Foundation of America in Washington, D.C., highly recommends it.
- Contact your local trade-promotion agency or state Department of Commerce to look into matchmaking programs.
- Find the hot trade leads by asking people in your industry. Also contact the Department of Commerce's country-desk officers, or place an ad in its monthly magazine, *Commercial News USA*.
- If you're targeting Japan, VentureLink USA (310-822-5628) helps U.S. companies do business there in areas such as product analysis, market research, advertising, and deal negotiation.

110
IDEA

Foreign Packing

I've seen Americans at overseas trade shows who can't find their products, who've lost their equipment, and whose people were held up at customs," says Keith Kiel, vice president of MacAcademy, a videotape distributor in Ormond Beach, Fla. He gives this **advice on what to bring (and what to leave at home)**:

- Copies of all documents. Kiel brings every fax he's received from the trade-show organizer. The paperwork can help smooth over situations where, for instance, you were promised audiovisual equipment and it's not there.

- A carnet. This detailed customs document listing all the valuables you take out of the States isn't required, but it can save you paperwork coming and going, and reduce the risk of being taxed on your own watch or luggage when you leave other countries.

- Half as much product and twice as many brochures as you think you'll need. Overseas customers respond better to a soft sell. They want a nice brochure to take home and study, which means fewer products sold at the show but more phone calls afterward.

- No equipment. Kiel rents everything, including computers and overhead projectors. He contacts manufacturers for the names of foreign distributors who can rent the equipment he knows he'll need. If there's no rental option, he always ships via the trade show's recommended carrier, even if it's more expensive than other carriers, because the recommended carrier usually can better help usher equipment through customs.

111
IDEA

Speaking in Tongues

Overseas trade shows can be valuable places to gather market research before trying to sell abroad—especially when language and cultural barriers loom.

After success selling his MacAcademy computer-training videos at shows in Canada, Singapore, and Hong Kong, Randy Smith, CEO of Florida Marketing International, tackled Europe. But his company was snubbed at an Amsterdam show; attendees bypassed its tapes, which were available in English only. "We knew **they'd rather have a product in their own language**," recalls Smith, "but we thought they'd buy the English one anyway."

For a year and a half he spent one week every other month at foreign shows with participants from up to 28 countries. After measuring the potential for sales of tapes in other languages, Smith decided to reshoot his videos as requested by target customers. He flew native-speaking teachers to Florida for filming, instead of dubbing or using bilingual Americans.

When MacAcademy attended Tokyo's MacWorld Asia show, the new tapes weren't yet available. But English language-tape sales were brisk, thanks to Smith's savvy offer to ship buyers the forthcoming Japanese version for free.

"Our philosophy has always been to compete with our competitors in their backyards. We feel that if we can compete effectively with Siemens in Germany, then surely we can compete with them in the United States or the rest of the world. But we have to wage battle on their home turf."

WILLIAM W. GEORGE
President and CEO of Medtronic, Inc.

112
IDEA

Go East—with Help from Japan

You could try to crack the Japanese market by yourself, or you could do what Poor Boy Manufacturing did: Accept free help from the Japan External Trade Organization (JETRO).

JETRO (http://www.jetro.org, 212-997-0400) offers a wide array of free services to American companies interested in exporting to Japan. With eight information centers in the United States, the government-sponsored agency's services range from product-specialization programs to export seminars and trade shows. Under the trade and product counseling programs, Japanese experts are posted to the United States to help identify potential exports to Japan.

Among JETRO's most useful programs is a **database that matches sellers with potential Japanese customers**. The database contains case studies and details on trade fairs, best-selling products, and import procedures. JETRO publishes numerous market reports, newsletters, magazines, and videos, as well.

Poor Boy Manufacturing president Cotton Harmon initially made contact with JETRO when he attended its Export-to-Japan seminar near his Florissant, Mo., facilities. Later, with the assistance of JETRO, Harmon engaged in discussions with three Japanese companies, one of which became an exclusive distributor for Poor Boy's fishing lures in Japan. Four years later, Poor Boy's sales there have grown from $3,500 to $235,000, accounting for at least one-half of the company's total revenues.

113
IDEA

Trade Mission Possible

In addition to loans, grants, and opportunities to introduce your products to other countries, some state commerce departments even **arrange trade missions** to introduce in-state business owners to foreign buyers. That's how Ronald Fink, president of RGF Environmental Group, broke into the Asian markets.

The West Palm Beach, Fla., manufacturer of water-treatment systems, along with nine other Florida CEOs, was invited to participate in an environmental trade mission to Taiwan and South Korea by Ray Reddish, senior management analyst at Florida's Department of Commerce. Reddish also arranged a grant, so the trip only cost RGF $3,000.

In one week, Fink met with 64 potential distributors lined up by Reddish. Shortly afterward, orders started coming in. Eighteen months later, Fink hired 14 employees to handle the new Asian business, which had reached $1 million.

114
IDEA

Testing Through Trade Shows

Gauge the international market's interest in your product—**introduce yourself at a foreign trade show** to see what happens. That's how MCT Industries got started in exporting.

The Albuquerque, N.M., company designs and manufactures Department of Defense ground support equipment, such as aircraft towbars, munitions trailers, and specialty adapters. Encouraged by the International Trade Administration (800-USA-TRADE), a division of the Department of Commerce, MCT decided to exhibit at the 1993 Paris Air Show to find potential clients and representatives for the Arab Gulf, Asia, and South America regions.

The contacts made there led the company to pursue the export market further and participate in other Department of Commerce shows in China, Taiwan, and Dubai. As a result, MCT increased its contacts in several Asian countries and netted a single area-exclusive representative for the Arab Gulf States.

115
IDEA

On the Road to Another Country

Jim Ake, founder of Electronic Liquid Fillers (ELF), an $18-million packaging-equipment company in LaPorte, Ind., **looks at foreign territory as just like selling in another state**. Jeff Ake, his son and international sales manager at the time, started cracking the Pacific Rim market the old-fashioned way: making cold calls, setting up appointments, and pounding the pavement.

After only two months' preparation, Jeff Ake spent seven weeks cold-calling 90 potential sales representatives and customers in the Pacific Rim. Ake obtained leads from foreign-based English-language trade magazines and faxed letters to about 400 prospects and reps to set up appointments. He left the country with only one-third of his time booked with appointments. The home office set up and confirmed more appointments for him while he was on the road, and Ake picked up the Yellow Pages to find other prospects to fill out his calendar.

Ake brought English-language videos for prospects and reps to pave the way for his visit. He also produced a brochure explaining why ELF was a good company to work with, including specification sheets of products, drawings, and press clippings.

On his Pacific Rim trip, Ake promised a 24-hour response time for price quotes—just as he does in the United States. He altered ELF's 10-day delivery promise only slightly for overseas customers: With a confirmed letter of credit, they could expect delivery in two to four weeks.

ELF's aggressive international approach paid off. The trip cost $19,000 and generated $2 million in sales.

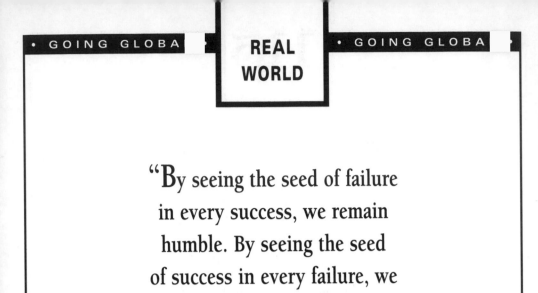

"By seeing the seed of failure in every success, we remain humble. By seeing the seed of success in every failure, we remain hopeful."

MEL ZIEGLER
founder of Banana Republic

116

IDEA

Send Your Services Abroad

The overseas market for professional services is alive and well, according to Jimmy Calano, CEO of CareerTrack, a business-seminar company in Boulder, Colo. Three years after starting to export its seminars, the company was pulling in 20% of its $52 million in revenues, and a slightly larger share of its profits, from abroad.

"We thought we'd have to tailor our examples to be country-specific," said Calano. "But most attendees preferred the American examples."

People in other countries turned out to be more responsive to direct marketing. On average, CareerTrack got approximately **50% more responses from an overseas mailing** than from the same mailing in the United States. To cut costs, CareerTrack bought mailing lists in foreign countries but did the data processing and printing at home. The finished materials were then shipped overseas for local mailing.

In many cases, foreigners were willing to pay more for the same product. So CareerTrack got at least as much revenue as it did in the United States at a lesser expense.

117
IDEA

Swap Contacts for Data

Export trading companies, which act as international distributors, have something novice exporters need badly: experience with international markets. But you don't have to give up total control to tap their expertise.

"Different export traders will provide different levels of service that can be negotiated," said Tom Erickson, CEO of the Chromaline Corp., a specialty-chemical company in Duluth, Minn. Once Erickson gained some overseas exposure, he was able to **win terms with traders that ran counter to the norm**.

When Erickson discovered H&H Exports, also in Duluth, he knew the trading company lacked experience with Chromaline's printing-industry clients. So he negotiated to give H&H his overseas prospects if H&H agreed to conduct market research and share the findings.

Under the terms of the agreement, Erickson accompanied the export trader on overseas visits, which built his contact database. At the same time, H&H Exports benefited from Erickson's introductions to existing clients and his knowledge of the industry. H&H Exports handled shipping, documentation, and delivery, and had ultimate control of pricing. Still, Erickson had access to the numbers. "It was difficult learning how to price," he admitted, "so our export trader really helped with that."

When Chromaline started exporting with H&H Exports, its sales were in the low six figures. Twelve years later, its sales had climbed to $7.5 million, one-third from overseas. The export trader's role later was scaled back to pursuing sales in Asia, but in the early days, Erickson reported, they had a close partnership in pioneering and developing markets, which was more effective in getting new customers.

118

IDEA

Taking the Transatlantic Plunge

f you think it's time to take your business overseas and if you're feeling burned out, consider letting one situation alleviate the other. That's what Dick Rubin did. When he decided to take Boston Metal Products global, he and his wife did it themselves—**by moving abroad**.

"I could have delegated the job to someone else," said Rubin, "but what would I be delegating? I didn't know anything about doing business in Europe. All I knew was that we belonged there, that there was a market for our products."

So Rubin and his wife moved to the Netherlands. Three years later, international sales accounted for about 20% of the Medford, Mass., company's revenues and an equal percentage of its profits. Along the way, Rubin made a discovery about what he calls "the power of the presidency."

"Everywhere I go, I run into middle managers of U.S. companies. I've yet to meet an American CEO. Evidently, people just don't realize the respect accorded presidents in Europe. It opens doors; it instills confidence that promises will be kept."

Rubin made a discovery about himself, too. "I took over my father's business in 1967. Today I feel as if my personal clock has gone back 23 years; I'm building something from scratch again, and I'm thriving on it. I feel revitalized."

119
IDEA

Cooking Up Sales

When you're selling to a foreign prospect, the pomp and circumstance of formal meetings may interfere with closing a deal. After years of selling internationally, Wayne Cooper decided to **balance the formality with an evening of decidedly casual entertaining**.

It began when Cooper, CEO of Arcon Manufacturing in Charlotte, N.C., invited a delegation from China to his ranch to cook up their own favorite dishes. "They had been on the road for a month and missed their native cuisine," explained Cooper.

Now he turns his kitchen over to visiting business travelers as often as once a month. Usually, the groups cook just for themselves, Cooper, and his wife, Judy. The emphasis is on socializing, but, of course, there's often a business payoff in the end. In the case of the Chinese delegation, Arcon, which builds grain silos, closed a sale the very next day that it had been negotiating for a year and a half.

VII

"Since the invention of the
microprocessor, the cost of moving a byte
of information around has fallen on the
order of 10-million-fold. Never before in
human history has any product or service
gotten 10 million times cheaper—much less
in the course of a couple of decades. That's
as if a 747 plane, once at $150 million
a piece, could now be bought for about
the price of a large pizza."

MICHAEL ROTHSCHILD
author of *Dionomics, Economy as Ecosystem*
(Henry Holt, 1990)

Siting Your Information

To keep Internet surfers coming back to your Web site again and again, put useful information there and keep it updated. Why? On the Internet, "content is king." If traditional advertising is 90% persuasion and 10% information, **effective Internet marketing is the other way around: 90% information and 10% persuasion**.

Elliot Rabin, president of Ridout Plastics (http://www.sddt.com/~plastics), has successfully built an Internet presence with this principle in mind. He created his Web site with $199 of authoring tools and began posting Ridout's entire corporate research library on it, along with information about the custom-designed plastic components and displays manufactured by his $7-million San Diego-based company.

Rabin then promoted his site, and the information it hosted, by listing it with all the major search engines. He spent about five hours a week requesting links with other sites related to plastics, and connected with several universities doing research on plastics.

Now, Ridout is *the* plastics Internet site. During the first eight months since his Web debut, 15% of Ridout's new business came from people who first encountered the company on the Web. Since then, the site consistently gets at least 20,000 hits each month. The site increased sales of his brochure holders by 50% with no additional marketing efforts, and it led to big contracts with national clients such as State Farm Insurance. With business expanding into 12 new countries overseas, Rabin believes his Internet efforts will continue to pay off.

Proper Netiquette

Soliciting customers through newsgroups—those thousands of electronic bulletin boards on the Internet—can be tricky because the vast majority ban commercial activity. Some groups allow notices like, "If you need a lawyer, call or e-mail me." Others treat unsolicited "spamming" with disdain and "flame" offenders with hostile e-mail.

The safest way to promote your company is to surf the bulletin boards relevant to your business, answer questions, and **post advertisements only to the newsgroups that accept ads**, such as alt.business.misc and biz.misc.

Rick Bell, president of Harvard Business Service (HBS), promotes his company by trolling newsgroups, responding to posted inquiries. HBS, a $2-million registered agent in Delaware that provides companies with incorporation services and helps them find venture capital, selects business and entrepreneurial newsgroups that are accessible to entrepreneurs worldwide.

Is it worth it? "Yes," says Bell. "Our volume has doubled in a year. The Internet is a way to reach millions of people, and it's very cost-effective. I don't know how we ever did things before."

122
IDEA

Web Bootstrapping

Drew Munster started his Web site with the same penny-pinching ethic he applied when he started his San Luis Obispo, Calif., direct-mail business, Tennis Warehouse. In six months he not only saved printing and postage costs but actually **expanded his catalog by building his own Web page**.

A few weeks of hypertext markup language (HTML) programming practice took just two additional weeks to roll out a basic 30-page electronic catalog listing all 1,000 of his products. About 200 items are hypertext-linked to color photographs and to text that details product features. Total cost: $430 a month. In the first six months he saved $1,000 over the cost of his old print catalog.

Munster paid a local service provider $30 a month to maintain his Web site and six e-mail accounts. In addition, Munster paid $150 a month for an advertising link from a popular tennis site to his site (http://www. tennis_warehouse.com/tw).

In one year his sales jumped from $250,000 to $750,000, and he credits the Web site with at least 25% of that growth. "We have all the business we can handle," Munster concluded.

123
IDEA

E-mail, or Else!

Some companies, who used to communicate with distributors, retailers, sales representatives, and suppliers by phone, fax, and mail, are discovering e-mail communication is a better way to go. In fact, Craig Aberle, president of MicroBiz, of Mahwah, N.J., demands it.

Get e-mail or get lost: This was the ultimatum issued by Microbiz, a software development company, to nearly 1,000 with whom it does business. About 95% of MicroBiz's $5 million in sales comes through resellers across the country. Aberle sent each a letter, saying, "We require all dealers to get on e-mail, or we won't give you any leads."

Initially, people grumbled. Within a few months, however, everyone was online. As a result, MicroBiz's **monthly phone bill has dropped** from $35,000 to $16,000. Now, rather than call resellers with leads, employees e-mail them. And dealers have started e-mailing one another with ideas and referrals.

124
IDEA

Honor Thy Neighbor

Everyone loves an award, especially if it can be posted on a Web site for others to see. If your organization has an authoritative position over an industry niche, you could honor Web sites related to your area of expertise to **build exposure and publicity for your own site**.

This worked for Scott and Sally Kiehnau of Reston, Va., who host GraphicLinx (http://www.graphiclinx.com), a site dedicated to promoting graphic design firms and service providers. Once a month GraphicLinx picks a site that excels in graphic excellence. "The winning site usually places the award on its Web page," says Sally Kiehnau, "and we end up with a banner ad on that site at no charge!" The time to administer the award and the Web site pays for itself in getting leads for their company.

Online Damage Control

Out of the Internet's thousands of newsgroups and mailing lists, many are devoted to specific industries, products, or services. With customers, suppliers, and competitors mixing it up online, there are plenty of opportunities to control damage, collect feedback, and provide support.

David Higgins, former research scientist for Invitrogen Corp., stopped potential negative word of mouth when he found a posting in a molecular biology newsgroup trashing one of his company products, a DNA cloning vector (a circular bit of DNA used in research). Higgins quickly fired off a response, identifying himself as an Invitrogen employee, and offered tips and published references on how to make better use of the product.

Jim Hoeffler, current director of R&D, says the Internet's unbounded ideas and opinions intensified Invitrogen's commitment to customer service. The $20-million, Carlsbad, Calif.-based manufacturer of gene expression kits and reagents regularly **scans relevant Usenet groups for messages about the company and its products**. Technical service representatives regularly check newsgroups that focus on molecular biology, looking for opportunities to help customers. Customers also contact Invitrogen by e-mail to receive support or learn about new products.

Information Exposure

Just about anyone can use free Internet newsletters and informational booklets to build credibility, exposure, and revenues.

Al Bredenberg **offers free Internet marketing articles on his Web page** (www. copywriter.com) and by e-mail autoresponder (a technology that automatically sends a prewritten response to an e-mail request). Bredenberg posts his offer to Internet newsgroup discussions, gets on e-mail discussion lists, and advertises his Web page.

Bredenberg promotes his $12 booklet, *The Small Business Guide to Internet Marketing,* in an electronic signature at the bottom of each e-mail and posting. In one year, the book sold more than 800 copies to users in 25 countries, and Bredenberg has grossed over $6,000 just in booklet sales.

The exposure he created on the Web has led to print exposure, too. He has been asked to write for *Internet World, Target Marketing, End-User Computing Management, Today's Homeowner, Web Marketing Today,* and other periodicals. But more importantly, the booklet sales and publicity have brought him new clients for his marketing and copywriting consulting business.

127
IDEA

Ambassadors with Netiquette

Paying cooperative third parties to recommend your Web page can produce hits. Just ask Ned B. Barnett, APR, senior vice president of Notch/Bradley, a healthcare-only advertising agency in Las Vegas. The key to being successful, he maintains, is to spread the word honestly, rather than sandbag the public with fluff.

When Barnett was promoting HealthWorld Online (www.healthy.net), he **hired knowledgeable third parties to post announcements to newsgroups**, or send e-mail to various lists, advocating some feature of the site. They did it in an informative, noncommercial way.

For example, college students with their own e-mail accounts posted noncommercial comments, such as: "My acupuncturist told me that the FDA was still trying to regulate her out of business. I wanted to know more—and find out what I could do about this—and I found my answers at the Legal and Legislative Forum in HealthWorld Online (healthy.net). You ought to check out this site."

Barnett recommends putting the right post in the right newsgroup, and making the announcement different in every newsgroup. Otherwise it looks like, and is, "spam" (the term for unsolicited advertising, which is frowned upon on the Internet).

Barnett's strategy is labor intensive, but it is very effective. His ambassadors' postings helped the site go from zero to 1.2-million hits per month in just six months; and in one controlled test, a single post to an America Online forum generated 30% of all site hits during the following week.

128
IDEA

Everybody Loves a Winner

Jackie Williams wanted to attract parents and nannies to her placement and recruiting company in West Hartford, Conn. When she launched the Web site for I Love My Nanny, she discovered that everybody loves an award winner.

After registering her site with several Web directories, Williams searched for parent-related or competing sites to see which ones rewarded other sites for design or information or had received such awards. Williams followed the award links to the organizations that gave them, and submitted her Web site for the same awards.

A few weeks later she received the "Best of the Net Award" from EZ Connect, and "Top Site Recruiter" from Net Temps. Her recognition then led to a Parent Soup "Souper Site" award and a "Top 5% of The Net" from Lycos. **The number of visitors to her Web site jumped with each award**, since the awarding site added a link to http://www.ilovemynanny.com.

Williams measures success by how long it takes her to answer e-mail from new customers. "Normally it takes two hours to answer e-mail," she says. "For about a week after I receive each award, it takes me about four hours. But I'm not complaining."

"People don't market their Web sites very well and then they end up disappointed with their lackluster results. It's sort of like selling into China for the first time: after its first year there, do you think Pepsi would have said: 'Well, we aren't doing that well so maybe we should ditch the country'? Of course not. Like China, the Internet is a huge new market. It's up to you to figure out what to do with it. Use it as a prospecting tool, make connections with people, add value for your existing customers. People are too darn myopic about making money and they get disappointed fast. If they haven't sold enough flowers they say: 'I'm out of here.'"

LARRY CHASE
president of Chase Online Marketing Strategies, New York, N.Y.
and at http://chaseonline.com

129
IDEA

Target Marketing via E-Zines

Although the Internet medium is new, the same print or direct-mail marketing rules still apply: **when online, market to a target audience**.

Once you decide who you want to reach online, find out what types of publications they're most likely to read, recommends Jim Daniels, who markets informational products on the Internet full-time. Then, focus on advertising in smaller publications like specialized on-line newsletters and magazines.

Daniels points to the response of an ad he ran in two on-line newsletters. Newsletter no. 1 had over 250,000 subscribers, and the response was three times that of newsletter no. 2. Even so, newsletter no. 1 resulted in only two sales. Newsletter no. 2 had a subscription base of only 8,000 but resulted in eight sales. Why were the results so different? The smaller publication was read by people interested in business-opportunity products. After just eight months online, Daniels managed to shed his day job to operate JDD Publishing (http://www.bizweb2000.com) from his Smithfield, R.I., home.

Daniels believes that the number of quality E-zines (on-line magazines) on the Internet is growing at a rapid pace, so finding five or six related to what you are selling should be relatively easy. One source of available E-zines can be found on the Web at (http://www.meer.net/~johnl/e-zine-list/).

130
IDEA

Chat Your Way to Business

Participating in Internet discussion groups is a great way to establish your reputation—and gain business—with a highly targeted group of prospects.

Case in point is Liz Seegert, a freelance writer and marketing consultant in Little Neck, N.Y., who discovered the **low-cost marketing benefits of on-line discussion groups** when she began exploring the world of cybermarketing in 1996.

Seegert is an active member of BizWomen (http://www.bizwomen.com), a women-in-business group, and ISBC, the International Small Business Consortium (http://www.isbc.com). Both groups' members include small and midsize business owners and managers—an ideal audience for her services.

When members post questions to the discussion boards, Seegert promptly answers those with issues that relate to marketing or business. Her signature file subtly points members to her Web site, where they can get more information about her services, monthly on-line newsletter, and general marketing issues.

"Sharing my knowledge with other group members lets them see that I know what I'm talking about when it comes to marketing issues." Seegert says. This has led to many inquiries and ultimately, several paying projects. The resulting business from discussion groups amounted to $6,000 in 1996, which she considers a great return for $480 a year in Internet access costs.

Sell Yourself with Your Signature

On the Internet, where massive amounts of information compete for a customer's attention, you need "secret weapons" to let people know about your products and services. The folks at BookZone, (http://www.bookzone.com), one of the oldest and busiest book sites, use the lowly "signature."

An e-mail signature is a small text blurb that automatically attaches to the end of your e-mail and newsgroup postings, allowing you to add information about your company, services, and products. This addendum helps **spread the word about your offerings without actually selling**. You can mention a special sale, promote a client, bolster your benefits, float a fresh idea, even if your message doesn't talk about your business at all.

Mary Westheimer, BookZone's president, not only mentions her company's services, she also changes her signature daily to promote BookZone's clients. Sales for those publishers have risen as much as 75% on the days their latest book title is part of her signature.

132
IDEA

Add Cybervalue to Your Proposal

Even if you're not in the Web design business, offer your Internet skills to new customers—and your company may benefit.

Paul L. Berg, CEO of Enterprise Builders, a $20-million construction company in Simsbury, Conn., not only knew a lot about building structures, he could also build Web sites. When bidding on a job to build a private school, Berg discovered that the school needed to raise funds to pay for the construction. So, he **included free Web-site design and hosting services in his bid**. Berg explained that the site could be used to attract fundraisers, and show alumni and contributors the results of their generosity. When school officials saw he had their interests in mind, they awarded him the contract. This added value made his proposal stand out from the competition.

It cost Berg $9 per month to rent space from a local Internet service provider and $100 to register his client's domain name. He spent one weekend designing the school's site, and half an hour every month to update it with the photos of the building's progress. The Web site accomplished two goals: It attracted funds for the school, which were necessary to pay Berg, and it showcased his construction work, both on land and on the Internet.

133
IDEA

Web Acrobatics

How do you make your most current marketing materials available to customers and partners immediately, in full color, with virtually no fulfillment costs? Just **convert your data files into Adobe Acrobat portable document format and post them on your Web site**.

That's how PID Inc.—a $10-million company headquartered in Phoenix, Ariz.—conveys its batch-automation software marketing information to its Fortune 500 customers. Robert Hylton, director of marketing for the company, uses Adobe Acrobat (http://www.adobe.com) to compress large graphic files of his marketing pieces into smaller files that anyone can read with Adobe's free Acrobat Reader software. Customers who fill out a short prospecting survey can download the files immediately from PID's Web site. Or, Hylton can e-mail the files directly to key customers, distributors, or employees worldwide.

In the first six months since the files were posted on the site, Hylton estimates that 2,000 prospects will have downloaded PID's marketing materials. Those leads should bring 20 qualified prospects into the sales process, which he expects will lead to over $1 million in sales.

134
IDEA

Virtual Chivalry

Parlay a small cry for help in cyberspace into a huge project. Just be the right person in the right newsgroup at the right time.

Benjamin Yoskovitz, vice president of sales and marketing for meep! media, Inc. (http://www.meep.com), a Montreal-based Internet and intranet consulting company, knew that one of the best ways to find new business was to **offer a hand to floundering prospects in Internet newsgroups**. When he came across a posting from a company looking for a small program in a hurry, Yoskovitz took on the small project; more important, he got his foot in the door.

The client asked for some minor changes and Yoskovitz obliged, with no additional charge. Meep! media was soon contacted again by the client, to work on a much larger project for the Canadian Government, worth 15 times as much as the first one, with more work likely to follow.

"The bottom line is that the opportunities are out there on the Internet," says Yoskovitz. "It's just a matter of looking in the right places—and being willing to start small."

Give Web Surfers a Wave

Give Web surfers information and entertainment, and the business will fall into your hands.

Michael Gellman, president of GIG Consulting, an Internet marketing/consulting firm in Denver, Colo., recommends that his clients **offer free services on their Web sites to bring in new leads and inquiries**. He practices what he preaches, implementing the same technique for his own company—a technique that caters to an upscale clientele usually unreceptive to free offers.

Gellman found that companies needed to evaluate the effectiveness of their Web sites from a marketing standpoint. To meet that need, he instituted a free Web-site review that allowed Web users to receive a comprehensive analysis of their content, design, and commercial dynamics. The cost was minimal and the results were remarkable.

Instead of the anticipated inquiries from small businesses and individuals with personal home pages, most requests came from international corporations that could utilize Gellman's services. Within a matter of months, GIG Consulting landed several major clients, and has now begun a major expansion.

VIII

"Advertising people who ignore
research are as dangerous as
generals who ignore decodes
of enemy signals."

DAVID OGILVY
Ogilvy on Advertising
(Vintage Books, 1985)

136
IDEA

Six Little Words

Make a practice of consistently asking each new customer this six-word question: **"How did you hear about us?"**

That's how Kevin Dueck, manager of WorkSpace Furniture in Soquel, Calif., determined which marketing methods were most effective for his business. Dueck and his employees query each new customer and record responses on a sheet behind the counter. What they have learned led to immediate changes in marketing strategy and focus which, he believes, helped WorkSpace grow 85% in the last six months of its first year.

When Dueck launched his store, he placed ads in several newspapers and put furniture in his parking lot only on special occasions. From his informal survey of customers, he concluded, "The majority of customers respond to the ad in one local newspaper, or they come in because they see the furniture and banners in our parking lot. Now, furniture is out every weekend, the banner stays up, and we've consolidated our advertising to one paper."

Use Customer Data

Paying attention to market research and using the data collected has made all the difference in the world to Katherine Barchetti, owner of a $3-million clothing and shoe store in Pittsburgh. A few years ago, Barchetti and her staff started analyzing a database into which her late husband had pumped 20 years of handwritten customer information, such as buying habits and fashion preferences, and **used the data to expand her product line and restructure personnel**.

Barchetti wrote letters to 3,000 people asking why they no longer shopped at her stores; 290 people wrote back. Although it took her a year and a half to reply to all of them, she quickly responded to their feedback by saying goodbye to an unfriendly manager and expanding her product line and price range.

A recent mailer to 5,000 top-spending customers brought in 181 shoppers, who purchased $90,000 worth of merchandise in one week—representing a 96% increase in total sales over the same week the previous year.

Barchetti's efforts resulted in a 12% increase in gross profits in the following year, faster inventory turnover, and more focused direct-mail campaigns.

138
IDEA

The Name Is the Game

When it comes to your company name, be choosy," advises marketing guru Jack Trout. "And remember, **the best names are locked directly to a product benefit or a selling proposition**." Here are some more of Trout's suggestions:

- *Simply describe what you're selling.* Your name is the first thing consumers know about you, so capture the idea in very simple terms, as Toys "R" Us and Guiltless Gourmet did.

- *Connect the name with the strategy.* A descriptive name like Lens Express tells consumers that the company is offering speedy contact-lens services. Just remember that you're committing yourself to whatever you say.

- *Steer away from generic names.* A big idea with a great name isn't enough. To compete, a company has to give customers a sense of why they're going into its store instead of someone else's.

- *Don't limit yourself.* Musical Chairs Ticket Service is a clever name, but it's focused solely on music and not on sports. While a brilliant name is important, it has to line up with your strategy.

139
IDEA

Marketing Under the Influence

You'd like industry authors, leaders, and speakers to act as influencers for your business. To find the people at the top of your word-of-mouth pyramid, you can start your own list using conference and trade show programs, Web pages, magazine articles, and books.

Rather than purchase a mailing list to plug her first book, *Taming the Recreational Jungle*, Silvana Clark dug up conference programs from shows she attended in the recreation field and sent for others she had missed. **Some conference organizers even gave her a list of the speakers**. Once she had the names and hometowns of these industry leaders, she used directory assistance and CD phone listings to obtain their phone numbers and addresses, then sent them the book.

Influencers may even become customers. Following one conference, Clark sent her usual cover letter and copy of the book to three speakers, all college professors. Each ended up ordering more than 100 books to use as supplemental textbooks for their recreation classes.

Surveying the Inactive

Interviewing inactive customers can be tough medicine, according to Bruce Grench, CEO of a small mail-order operation in Olivette, Mo. But it works.

Grench, owner of HDIS, a 40-employee provider of personal-care products, takes several approaches—including **in-home focus groups**—to solicit comments from would-be, current, and lost customers. "The hope," he says, "is that we can find something we're not doing right, because it offers us an opportunity."

HDIS responded to price-conscious customers by introducing a line of private-label products, which now account for 15% of the business. Grench notes that a spoonful of sugar helps bitter medicine go down. By surveying many of his customers, he hears from a lot who are happy. That, he says, "was our ulterior motive."

141
IDEA

Hire Undergraduates, Get Educated

Seventy-three percent of Illinois independent retailers rated themselves poor to fair at gathering customer information, according to *Small Store Survival,* a study and report by Arthur Andersen & Co. and the Illinois Retail Merchants Association (800-572-5044, $90, 322 pages). Beth Willey, co-owner of Henderson's Department Store in Sycamore, was in that category. But she didn't have time to research her market, or a lot of money to pay for it.

So, Willey **hired aspiring marketing students to do her market research**. At $5 per hour, two enthusiastic college undergraduates designed a questionnaire and polled 1,200 of her customers, using a mail-in survey. For the cost of printing, postage, and $80 in labor, Willey received back 592 completed three-page questionnaires. The research concluded that she needed to target a younger market and provide better service. Willey adds, "The survey also increased the awareness in our product mix so we carry less of items that don't sell."

Woo the Unresponsive

In customer-service circles, no news is bad news. That's why Ruppert Landscape makes sure to **contact customers who don't respond** to its twice-a-year customer-satisfaction surveys.

Sixty percent of Ruppert's 800 accounts give the company high marks. It's the 40% who don't respond that cause management to worry. "We assume the worst," says vice-president Chris Davitt. "Those customers could be about to leave, and we need to reach them. We send a follow-up letter that yields another 15%." A manager visits or phones the remaining 25% and those who gave Ruppert a negative report. It's time-consuming, but it pays off in increasingly larger renewal contracts and fewer bad debts.

"The ability to 'listen in' on conversations about you or your competitors may represent one of the best market-research values of the Internet, simply because it's unique to the medium. I'm talking, of course, about the newsgroups and discussion groups so prevalent in the Usenet section of the Internet."

SUSAN GRECO
articles editor, *Inc.* magazine, http://www.inc.com

143
IDEA

Sample the Competition

Allen Susser, owner of Chef Allen's, a $3-million restaurant in North Miami Beach, Fla., checks on his competitors and keeps his employees involved in his restaurant, for no more than the price of a meal. How? He encourages employees to eat at other restaurants and report back on their experience.

Chef Allen's started a program Susser calls "Chow Now." **Each employee gets $50 to dine at any restaurant** with cuisine similar to Chef Allen's. Employees return with short written and oral reports on what they learn. Nearly all staffers participate—at a rate of two or three a month.

When a cook for Chef Allen's sampled a competitor's fare, he was dismayed to find elegant food being served on cold plates. It ruined the meal, he reported at a staff meeting. "He thought more about warming up plates after that," says Susser. "They like to laugh at the little mistakes and believe they wouldn't make them."

It must be working. Chef Allen's consistently receives rave reviews for food and service, and employee turnover is low. And, reports Susser, Chow Now has boosted employee morale.

144

IDEA

Develop Customer Ideas

For many companies, a difficult business hurdle is inventing a product that customers will buy. At Paper Direct, a subsidiary of the Deluxe Corp., nobody worries about where the next hit product will come from. The St. Paul, Minn., business, which sells direct marketing specialty papers via catalog, **counts on customers for great ideas**.

Six times a year, Paper Direct's "Show Us Your Stuff" contests yield up to 300 suggestions per campaign, up to 10 of which lead toward new product developments. "People were always sending in unsolicited ideas," recalls Raleigh Koritz, manager of public relations. "We thought we'd reward them for their efforts."

The top entries win money (the first prize is $500 in company credit; runners-up get $50) and fame in the catalog's feature, "Show Us Your Stuff."

145
IDEA

May I Borrow Your Expert?

Can't afford a marketing staff? Borrow one, the way Tom Klein did. The CEO of $25-million NorthWord Press, a book and audio products publisher in Minocqua, Wis., **asked six marketing pros from other companies to be his advisers**. At quarterly brainstorming sessions, the advisers weigh strategic issues such as pricing and product development. Their feedback helped NorthWord drop a line of books at odds with its market niche.

A former marketer of health-care products chairs the group, which includes a veteran market researcher and four customers from key distribution channels. All live within driving distance and were flattered to be asked to help. Klein pays each a small per diem and hotel expenses for a total cost of $10,000 a year. However, Klein says, "I need only one product idea to cover the costs." His total marketing budget is 1% of sales—half of what's typical for a small company.

Impersonate a Competitor

If you're not sure whether your customers are happy with you, one creative way to find out is to impersonate a competitor.

Michael LeBoeuf, author of *How to Win Customers and Keep Them for Life,* tells the story of a conversation one pharmacist overheard when a teenage boy entered a drugstore phone booth: "Hello, is this the Smith residence?...I would like to apply for the opening you have for a gardener...What's that, you already have a gardener? Is he a good gardener? Are you perfectly satisfied with all of his work?...Is he not doing anything that you would like to have done?...Do you plan on keeping him?...I see...Well, I'm glad you're getting such excellent service. Thanks anyway. Bye."

As he left the booth the druggist remarked, "Johnny, I couldn't help overhearing your conversation. I know it's none of my business, but aren't you the Smiths' gardener?" To which Johnny replied, "That's right. **I just called to find out how I'm doing**."

147 IDEA

Quick Reaction

It might not be polished, but **fast, informal feedback from potential customers** is better than no feedback at all—especially when you're considering launching a new product and want to see whether there's any market for it at all.

When Randy Amon and a friend were first deciding whether to quit their jobs and start a business, they implemented what they recall fondly as "the market-research minute": they called up one computer store. "We asked, 'If we made a cable that connected opposing equipment, would you buy it?'" Amon remembers.

Not only did the store say it would buy the cable, it placed an order over the phone. Amon didn't even have a company yet, or a product. The store said it would pay $35 apiece for five cables, so the budding entrepreneurs went out with $100 and bought the materials to make them.

The market research even mutated into training: "The customer showed me how to make the cable," says Amon. That launched ABL Electronics, now of Hunt Valley, Md., and a veteran of the *Inc.* 500.

148
IDEA

Artful Response to Customer Profile

For six weeks Mac McConnell, former owner of Artful Framer Gallery in Plantation, Fla., asked **walk-in customers to fill out a one-page questionnaire**. The survey polled customers on who they were, where they'd heard about Artful Framer, and how they rated the store's custom framing. While 85% of the shoppers gave the framing an excellent rating, their priorities list surprised McConnell. Quality won first place, uniqueness second place, and price was dead last. Instead of rushing out and raising prices, McConnell reinvented his business to satisfy customers' desires. Since they were clamoring for quality, he found the courage to abandon the low end and make museum framing his standard.

According to the survey, word-of-mouth brought in a third of his customers, so he gave people more reasons to tell their friends about Artful Framer. He added a lifetime guarantee on all work and started calling customers a month after purchase to see if they were satisfied.

About 80% of the customers surveyed checked off a household income of $40,000 or more. So, McConnell taught his salespeople to take a consultative approach to selling to the affluent crowd: First talk about where the customer plans to hang the art, then talk price.

A year after introducing the changes, the store's average invoice rose from $67 to $167. Over four years, overall sales tripled, to about $600,000, and net profits were up 26%.

Five-Dollar Research

What would you pay for a tactic that gets new customers into your store, gives you an **unbiased report on your company's service**, and brings you lots of new ideas? Gary Cino, CEO of 98¢ Clearance Centers in Sacramento, thinks it's worth at least five dollars.

When Cino meets someone who's never set foot in one of his 55 retail stores, where every item costs 98 cents, he hands the prospect an envelope. Inside is $5 cash to spend at his store, another envelope stamped and addressed to Cino, and a single-sheet questionnaire with a dozen queries such as "Did the cashier greet you at time of checkout?" The first-timers also rate the store's appearance and products, and provide comments and suggestions. Paid-up customers are also asked to attach a copy of their cash-register receipt.

"We're bribing them, but it's a relatively inexpensive way to accomplish a lot of things," says Cino, whose stores gross almost $100 million annually. He and his executives pass out some 500 packets a year, amounting to a measly $2,500 cash expense. About 85% of the shoppers return the survey within 90 days and spend more than their five dollars. Responses are posted at each store.

The envelope-and-cash technique is better than using mystery shoppers, says Cino. "We get more accurate information, and the respondents match our demographics." As for feedback, Cino decided to accept personal checks because so many survey participants mentioned they'd like that payment option.

Dig Through Your Documents

Want to increase your chances of **reaching the right potential customer**? Try digging through your company's receipt files for names. Documents including purchase orders, invoices, and receipts can identify who's likely to buy from you, where you're making the most money, and what product lines or types of business you should drop.

Joan V. Silver, president of Reeves Audio Visual Systems, started by sorting through her receipts to discover who was in the market for a $16,000 video-projection system. She found that some people knew Reeves for its service work, while others only purchased equipment.

Knowing this gave Silver a blueprint for creating a more effective marketing plan. First she started classifying the kinds of things her customers were and weren't buying from her. Then she tailored letters to each group, underscoring the company's full-service capabilities.

The results were clear. She could execute more targeted mailings once a month for the same cost as the big, unfocused quarterly mailings she used to do, and her response rate went up 10%.

"You can't just ask customers what they want and then try to give that to them. By the time you get it built, they'll want something new. It took us three years to build the NeXT computer. If we'd given customers what they said they wanted, we'd have built a computer they'd have been happy with a year after we spoke to them— not something they'd want now."

STEVE JOBS
former CEO of NeXT Computer
(bought by Apple Computer)

Distinctive, Relevant Incentive

How do you get people to fill out and send in questionnaires? **Keepsakes can work better than cash incentives**, since perceived value, rather than actual value, often means more to people.

Burke & Towner Ltd., a marketing communications company in Milwaukee, Wis., felt it was not getting its buck's worth from the $1 cash incentive it was sending with questionnaires to top health and education administrators. Searching for a premium that would make a greater impression, the firm settled on the Flexgrip ballpoint pen with a unique design. The pen could also be used to complete the questionnaire, so it was relevant to the project at hand.

Returns were 32% higher from this survey than from a similar study previously mailed with the standard $1 incentive. Since purple ink was selected for the pens, it was obvious to Burke and Towner that the vast majority of the recipients used their gifts to supply hard-to-get answers about goods and services. Some even used the pens to jot short, personal thank-you notes for the thoughtful present.

Zero in On Your Market First

One of the best—and most obvious—marketing advantages is to have a large pool of prospects who need your solution. Companies that don't do their homework spend thousands of dollars on product development and marketing, only to discover that no one wants their product.

Anthony Blake, a marketing consultant and entrepreneur from Ventura, Calif., decided not to make this mistake before writing *Inside Secrets of Incredible Super Sex.* Because he planned to sell his book via direct mail, Blake looked for suitable **mailing lists that were available for rent** in Standard Rate and Data Service's (SRDS) *Direct Mail List and Data.*

He spent about four hours at his local library with the SRDS book and found 15 lists, a total of 10 million people, who had bought sex-related products or books. The directory even told him the average expenditure and order-placing response time from each list. For example, Rodale Press, publishers of *Men's Health* magazine and health-related books, offered a list of 1.5 million names, half of whom had bought Rodale's book *Secrets of Men's Sex* in the previous 90 days.

Once Blake knew there was a market, he sent a direct-mail piece to some of the lists he had found, and advertised in publications that complemented his product. In 15 months Blake sold more than 12,000 copies of his book for $19.97 each, at an advertising and fulfillment cost of only $2.25 each.

153
IDEA

Get the Skinny on Best Customers

Every company wants to **target lifelong customers**. But how does a retailer identify this group? Health Valley, a producer of nonfat foods in Irwindale, Calif., couldn't survey all its supermarket customers but learned how to spot its strongest allies. The company identified them in two ways: One, those who saved up 20 bar-code labels for a $5 rebate. Two, those who ordered Health Valley's books: the $14.95 *Cooking Without Fat* or the $12.95 *Baking Without Fat*.

Along with the bar code and book offers on all products, Health Valley created a Preferred Customer Club. To track its preferred customers, Health Valley dedicated a toll-free line for their dietary questions. "When they call, we know something about them," said advertising director Harry Urist. Preferred customers also receive periodic product samples and newsletters in the mail.

Concocting a book of tasty, fat-free recipes was a nightmare, Urist admits. But the alternatives were unappetizing. Health Valley tried free-standing inserts in major Sunday newspapers. While a regular Sunday newspaper insert generated a 2% response, Health Valley's own newsletter yielded a stockier coupon-redemption rate. 8%. The best way to advertise, Urist concluded, was direct contact with customers.

154
IDEA

Make Your Survey a Game

Marketing vice-president Karen Schultz was well aware that her target customers were unemployed, immature, and capricious. She considered this peculiar situation perfectly normal, though. Her software company, KidSoft, published a quarterly magazine and CD-ROM for children, ages 4 to 14.

Schultz needed to find a way to elicit meaningful feedback from children, whose opinions of "cool" are always in flux. "If kids don't like what we feature, they aren't going to ask their parents for it," she says. To research her market, she **developed a survey so entertaining its young readers couldn't resist completing it**.

KidSoft used the Mad Libs fill-in-the-blank format to make the questionnaires fun for kids and a source of marketing data for the company. "When kids look at a normal questionnaire with its little cubes and boxes, they're not intrigued," Schultz explained.

Her response rate of 5% to 6% was "decent when you know that 2% to 3% is considered good for any general direct-marketing response." Overall, Schultz was satisfied that the kids wouldn't tire of completing Club KidSoft's surveys. Her certainty derived from readers like 13-year-old Shannon Manessis of Pinole, Calif., who completed the sentence "I think it would be great if you had..." with an appeal for "more forms to fill out like this."

155
IDEA

Appeal to Appetite

Getting customers to complete questionnaires can be difficult, if not impossible, even when you have the right people in front of you. What's the solution? **Improve questionnaire response**—try bribing them with candy. It works.

CME, producer of continuing medical education courses, has unique opportunities to poll large groups of physicians as they attend week-long classes. Unfortunately, they weren't turning in their completed surveys. Responses were ranging around 2%. So, Don Green, general manager for CME, decided to take advantage of their fatigue, offering them a Snickers "energy break" if they turned in their completed forms.

Between the lure of free, instant gratification and the poor alternatives on the refreshment tables, the docs fell for it. Responses went through the roof, averaging 75% of the surveys completed and returned.

Please Leave a Message

Here's a way to get customers to speak their minds: **set up a 24-hour hotline to record confidential messages**. Give the hotline a folksy name and promote it on company stationery, invoices, and "How'd-We-Do?" cards.

AVCA, a $50-million engineering and architectural service firm near Toledo, Ohio, did just that and received a positive customer response to the hotline. Several of AVCA's active clients telephoned Speakline, often to leave project-related questions. They also inquired about bills, made suggestions, and praised jobs well done. The line was especially convenient for customers who didn't have time to write, didn't know who should field their questions, and didn't want to play telephone tag.

AVCA president Dean Diver monitored the messages, which were recorded on an inexpensive answering machine. If he couldn't get back to a customer within 24 hours, he sent a note to explain. AVCA started Speakline because of the response from customer comment cards. Diver said, "We received a 35% return rate on those cards, so we knew many of our customers wanted to talk."

IX

"If you break the rules, you're going to stand a better chance of breaking through the clutter than if you don't. If you try to live with the rules, in all likelihood the work will be derivative, it won't be fresh, it won't have the necessary ingredients to disarm the consumer, who increasingly has got his defenses up against all sorts of advertising messages coming his way."

TOM MCELLIGOTT
Fallon, McElligott agency

Proof of the Pudding

Customers meet your marketing communications before they see your product or experience your service. So, **try a marketing strategy that exemplifies your highest-quality work**. For example, a graphic design firm would create an elegant brochure. A Web designer's home page would include outstanding technologies and graphics. A packaging firm could build a unique container to hold its marketing materials. And a public relations agency could seek publicity through a unique campaign.

When Deborah Mersino founded Paragon Public Relations in Evanston, Ill., she sent 120 press releases to business editors nationwide, stating that her company wanted to honor "an unknown entrepreneur." Entrants had to explain, in five sentences or less, why they deserved to be selected. The winner would receive a $5,000 six-month contract and the runner-up a $1,500 contract, with Paragon.

Mersino's campaign caught the attention of three newspapers, a magazine, and every radio station in Chicago. As a result 69 entrepreneurs entered the contest, which cost her only time and postage. For Paragon, the payoff was lots of press and instant credibility as a new agency.

158

IDEA

Confidence Artist

Let your customers know how confident you are about the quality of your product or service. It will instill confidence in them, too. Here's how some businesses can **communicate the value and quality of a product or service**:

- Caterer: Print a favorite recipe on business cards.
- Bakery: Print commitment to natural ingredients on the carry-out bags.
- Nursery: Distribute a pamphlet explaining the care and feeding the plants receive.
- Computer retailer: Publish an easy-return policy with a guide for sending back defective products.
- Clothing manufacturer: Use the hang tag to describe both a commitment to quality of the fabric and a special feature, such as a stronger seam that won't rip.
- House-cleaning business: Provide a detailed checklist of every service performed.
- Clothing retailer: Call all new customers to ensure complete satisfaction with their purchases.

Wear Your Product Like a Badge

Want to start sales-making conversations at business or social events without saying a word? Replace your attendee name tag with **a custom badge that advertises—maybe even looks like—your business or product**.

Terri Lonier, author of *Working Solo* and *The Frugal Entrepreneur,* buys pin backs from craft supply stores, tapes them to a laminated color laser print of her book cover, and wears them at trade shows. Lonier handed them out at one show to selected colleagues and friends who promised to wear them while walking the aisles. Soon people were saying, "Wow, I've seen that pin everywhere at the show!"

Marcia Yudkin, a Boston-based consultant and author of *Persuading on Paper,* uses a similar three-by-four-inch laminated pin to present her new book to everyone who walks by. The pins, which cost her a trip to Kinko's and $2.50, help sell an average of four books at each event she attends.

160
IDEA

Cost-Cutting Catalog Production

The co-owners of Pittsburgh-based Little Earth Productions, a $3.4-million wholesaler of recycled fashion accessories, are pros at getting bargains. Rob Brandegee and Ava DeMarco apply the same frugal approach to producing their four-color catalog as they do to reusing materials.

Little Earth publishes more than 30,000 business-to-business catalogs per year, but it **doesn't spend a fortune to create fancy pages**. For one issue, Brandegee talked a Miami photographer into doing work in exchange for the trip, the clips, and the references. Instead of hiring professional models, the company used its own employees and people on the street to show off its products. Little Earth approached two clothing wholesalers, and asked to use the wholesalers' clothing line in exchange for mentioning them in the catalog. DeMarco and Brandegee also got the wholesalers to foot part of the production bill.

Little Earth's cost-cutting production strategy has not prevented it from creating sharp catalogs that make sales. During the company's first year in business, its black-and-white catalog cost $14,000 and sold $120,000 worth of merchandise.

Million-Dollar Mailing

Would your prospects turn down the chance to win a million dollars? Dave Murphy, president of Murph's Productions, an advertising firm in Lewis Center, Ohio, doesn't think so. His prospects open their doors when he **adds a Lotto ticket to his flyer**.

A third of the way down the flyer he sends to prospects is a Lotto ticket, glued onto the flyer with text beside it that reads: "This ticket could be worth a fortune." Murphy glues his business card further down the page, and adds supporting text: "This is just the ticket to make you a fortune!" The bottom of the page reads: "The choice is yours! Don't take chances with your advertising...it's time to call Murph's!"

Murphy sent out just 36 flyers and obtained 22 qualified appointments—a 61% response rate. Since then, he has not had to use the promotion again. "I am still doing a mountain of business from the eight new clients I got from the 22 appointments," says Murphy.

The Annual Report Advantage

Here's a new argument for opening your company's books: it's a marketing tool. Unipower, an electronics manufacturer in Coral Springs, Fla., has discovered just how advantageous it can be for a private operation to **publish its annual report**.

The annual report details sales, number of employees, orders, net income, and balance-sheet information. But the real meat, according to marketing chief Ed Schneider, is a four-page section called "Understanding Unipower" that lists the company's markets, sales channels, competitors, and top 25 customers.

Why go to such lengths? "It tells our customers they're doing business with a real company," explains Schneider. "They can look at the sales history and say, 'Wow, they're growing, and they have inventory under control.'" He adds, "We want to impress customers and intimidate our competition. Everyone is teaming up with a limited number of suppliers. You have to set yourself apart." In the four years since it published its first annual report, Unipower grew 933%.

163 IDEA

Picture This: Less Is More

Magazine covers sell magazines, and book covers sell books—why not use the cover of your brochure to "sell" brochures? You'll save on costs, and **you'll be sending complete brochures only to prospects who really want to read them**.

For Saul Rowen, executive director of Cali-Camp Summer Day Camp in Topanga, Calif., one picture was worth a thousand words or, more accurately, $23,000. To cut costs, instead of sending out 16-page brochures that cost 72 cents a piece to produce and mail, Rowen sent just the brochure cover with photos of camp life, and a response card to request a complete brochure. At a cost of 43 cents a package, this practice saved 40% of the cost for brochures.

"We're saving money, and we're hitting our exact market," said Rowen, whose mailing to 46,000 prospects yielded 23 new campers worth $1,000 a head.

If You've Got It, Flaunt It

Direct mailers often **add a "teaser" on the envelope** to let prospects know what's inside, enticing them to open it. Other business mail—such as letters, invoices, thank-you notes, and so on—is not sent in these advertising envelopes. But if it were, people would sit up and take notice.

If you add an advertisement or message to your general-purpose envelope, every time you mail correspondence, the recipient's first impression will take in more than your return address. You can print a slogan when you address the envelope on your laser printer, or typeset a permanent message when your stationery goes to press.

Barbara Hoberman Levine, author of *Your Body Believes Every Word You Say* (Aslin Publishing, 1991), created custom envelopes with the title of her book on the front. "It didn't cost extra, and you never know who will see it," she says. This and other efforts spread word-of-mouth for the book, which has been a best-selling title for more than five years.

Everyone Takes Orders

When your staff is small, there's no reason why everyone can't take customer calls and fill out an order form. That way, if your salespeople are out or busy, a customer won't slip through the cracks. When Gus Blythe, president of SecondWind, a Paso Robles, Calif., retailer of athletic-shoe-care products, first started, his goal was to **turn every employee into an order taker**.

His simple step: Blythe hung order forms from each desk at the company. That way, he says, when the phone rings, there is no excuse not to take an order. The forms are self-explanatory, and every employee is capable of filling them out. "There's nothing worse than making a customer wait to give you money," says Blythe.

"Written reports
stifle creativity."

H. ROSS PEROT
American computer entrepreneur
and politician

Customer-Based Communications

When you sell a no-nonsense product like building materials, do you ask customers how your printed communications affect your image and relationship with them? Or are you just beaning them with a two-by-four?

Michael Harris, CEO of Deck House, a manufacturer of prefabricated post-and-beam house kits, decided to find out what customers thought. He **invited customers to an in-house meeting** at his offices in Acton, Mass., where they met employees from throughout the company.

After the meeting, he pinned all customer feedback to a bulletin board. Most comments centered on the confusing sales follow-up after a prospect called the company. "Here we were, asking intimate design questions, and then sending out curt invoices. We needed to be more personable," Harris says.

So, the accounting department reworded the invoices, and Harris developed a comprehensive resource book for new clients, detailing the design and building process, manufacturer referrals, and warranty information. Harris estimates the books cost $3 each, but it's worth spending a few thousand for customer goodwill. "We get lots of customer feedback, and they bring dog-eared copies to meetings," he reports.

The result: customer-survey ratings climbed. "Everyone," Harris says, "got to appreciate the customer's point of view."

Make Marketing an Inside Job

Put your outside marketing campaign to double use by using it to market inside your company as well," suggests Mary Stewart, president of Mary Stewart Written Communications in Portland, Ore. Your marketing materials are where your promises are made. If you **include your staff in the development of your materials, and show employees what goes out to customers**, they will take pride in living up to those promises.

Stewart suggests several ways to accomplish this:

- Include as many employees as possible in the data-collection process for these materials, then be sure they are well communicated throughout the company.
- Introduce marketing materials at staff meetings, and circulate them with quarterly status reports.
- Include marketing materials in the introduction of your employee handbook.
- Show the employees marketing pieces with the same sense of pride and enthusiasm that you convey to clients.

"Every product we put out has our Web address on it. Every direct marketing piece sent out has the address, and it's also on our phone line. Whenever we promote anything, the Web address is there. The cost? Absolutely nothing. Just type."

FAITHE RAPHAEL
vice president of strategic marketing,
Windham Hill Records

168
IDEA

Signature Font

Thousands of computer fonts are available to shape the style, mood, and readability of a printed piece. But only one font can translate your most personal touch—your own handwriting font. Signature Software (800-925-8840) takes a form that you fill out with handwritten letters and sends back a one-of-a-kind computer font in your handwriting.

You can use your signature font to add personalization to your materials in several ways:

- ❧ Add a personal note as a P.S. or in the margins of a sales letter.
- ❧ Automate bulk-mail envelopes that look hand-addressed.
- ❧ Add a "handwritten" memo or lift letter to a direct-mail piece.
- ❧ Make faxes from the computer look personal.
- ❧ Print thank-you notes, post cards, and personalized holiday cards.

What's on the Back?

Watch what happens when you hand out your business card. Often the recipient looks at both sides. What's on the back of yours?

The **reverse side of your business card** is an opportunity to say something more to your prospects and clients. Use this space for information about your product, a map to your location, or a special offer that your clients can use. For example, Stew Leonard, owner of a world-famous supermarket, gives out a card that includes a coupon for a free ice cream cone in his store. Most Japanese cards have directions on how to find the company's office in Tokyo.

You can also use the reverse side of your card to add a memorable message that makes your card, and you, stand out. Christina Eriksson, a Swedish advertising consultant, prints on the back of her card: "Women are born leaders. You have just met one." Blaine Greenfield, a Bucks County Community College professor and marketing consultant in East Windsor, N.J., prints "Important Telephone Numbers" on the back of his card. Greenfield lists the phone numbers for Boris Yeltsin, Bill Clinton, Pope John Paul, and himself—in boldface.

Need Sales? Write a Book

If your product is revolutionary and requires educating the market, you might take the approach of Dr. Matthias Rath, who **wrote a book to sell vitamins**.

Dr. Rath discovered that animals don't get heart attacks because they produce their own vitamin C. His research led him to formulate a daily vitamin supplement that was clinically tested and shown to reduce the risk of heart disease naturally. However, if he simply put his vitamins on the market with no supporting evidence of their benefits, skeptical consumers would reject the product as if it were snake oil. So, Dr. Rath set out to self-publish a book that would explain his discovery in lay terms, describe the daily regimen, and ultimately sell his product.

It took him two months to write *Why Animals Don't Get Heart Attacks...But Humans Do*. In two years, 150,000 copies of the $7.95 book were sold through his San Francisco-based company, Health Now. In Germany, it sold 30,000 copies in six months. The book not only made money and supported Rath's research, it also converted readers into customers. Ninety percent of readers ordered Health Now vitamins from the business reply card that was included in each copy.

171
IDEA

Flighty Ad, Soaring Response

Who in their right mind would send a paper airplane to serious prospects? Jacobs/Gillen—an advertising agency in Mason Neck, Va.—that's who.

Cofounder Mary Gillen's **most successful direct-mail campaign consisted of a simple red paper airplane** that had information and text printed in one color. The prospects had to unfold the airplane to read the message, part of which said, "If you would like to keep the cost of your advertising, copywriting, and graphics from soaring into the stratosphere, give us a call today. We'll keep your budget on the ground."

"We appealed to the 'kid' in these adults, and we hit a nerve," says Gillen. "The phone started ringing with people making airplane sounds, as they told us how much they loved it." Gillen pulled in a 7% response and five new clients.

172
IDEA

Marketing the Marketer

What marketing strategy does a marketing consultant use to get business? For Dave Voracek, founder of the Marketing Department, in Alexandria, Va., newsletters are the way to go.

Voracek sends a two-page newsletter to 120 clients and 280 prospects. He publishes marketing ideas, success stories, and a list of recent projects which remind clients of the variety of services he has to offer. "I also added my picture to the newsletter," says Voracek. "At first I thought it was vain, but I realized people remember me as the guy with short hair and glasses." Voracek prints extra copies to give away at conferences and networking events.

Right after the newsletter is mailed, Voracek receives two or three calls. The publication also prompts his friends and suppliers to refer business to him. For $250 per issue, which covers printing and postage, **the newsletter has landed four to five new clients a year**. For Voracek, it is the best return on his investment.

IDEA

Connection in the Cards

I f hands-on plant managers and shop engineers see my title, they think I'm a big-shot office guy who doesn't know what's going on in the marketplace," said Phil Pachulski, CEO of a $33-million distributor of machine tools based in Grand Rapids, Mich. **To avoid intimidating prospects on sales calls, he kept titleless business cards on hand**.

Pachulski also understood that, at times, a title is impressive. When he called on big-company employees to whom organizational charts are important, he gave them a card with his title on it and, *voilà*, instant rapport.

Picture Your Reputation

There was a good reason why New Pig Corp., a manufacturer of oil-absorbent socks for heavy machinery, put a **picture of its factory on every sales brochure**. A few salespeople reported that the competition was besmirching New Pig's reputation. "Somebody said we were a two-bit operation dragging in imports from Mexico," recalled one employee.

"We'll show them who has the biggest smokestack in town," said founder and chairman Don Beaver. To quiet skeptics, chairman Don Beaver placed a color photo of the New Pig factory in Altoona, Pa., on his brochure. From there on in, prospective customers had little doubt about New Pig's stature.

365 Reminders

Why is a calendar such a great business gift? Because it impresses your clients every day and month of the year. Career Blazers, a full-service staffing and training company headquartered in New York City, creates **calendars that are specific and unique to their corporate customers**.

Each month features a humorous cartoon related to human resources. But the calendars do more than keep the company name in front of existing clients and new prospects—they help bring back lost clients. "Of all lost clients or dropped prospects who don't get the calendar, 92% ask for one in a subsequent year," Lewis says. "This gives us another opportunity to re-establish the relationship." It's these relationships that have helped Career Blazers grow at the rate of approximately 40% per year.

"The key word is flexibility, the ability to adapt constantly. Darwin said it clearly. People thought that he mainly talked about survival of the fittest. What he said was that the species that survive are usually not the smartest or the strongest, but the ones most responsive to change. So being attentive to customers and potential partners is my best advice—after, of course, perseverance and patience."

PHILIPPE KAHN
founder of Borland International
and Starfish Software

176
IDEA

Put Prospects in the Picture

When customers are mulling over a big-ticket purchase, you can make the decision a little easier by **giving them a Polaroid snapshot of the product** they're considering. That's what Domain home-furnishing stores, based in Norwood, Mass., did. Salespeople for the company provided photos and wrote their names and the product on the reverse. Founder and CEO Judy George said that the photos helped customers feel more comfortable choosing Domain's furniture because they could compare it with products at other stores and with their own home furnishings.

Customers were also more inclined to keep the snapshot—and thus the salesperson's name and the product name—than a business card. "It helped them feel secure with the purchase and bonded them with the salesperson," said George. Bottom line: the low-cost practice increased Domain's sales-closing rate by 25%.

Six-Sentence Plan

Is your comprehensive marketing plan keeping you on track—or is it collecting dust? Marketing plans are supposed to keep your company focused, but many companies write the plan just to obtain funding and never look back.

Jay Conrad Levinson, author of the *Guerrilla Marketing* series of books, suggests **simplifying the marketing plan to six or seven sentences** that can be clearly communicated to your employees, suppliers, investors, board members, and marketing partners. Here's a hypothetical example of a company called Peak Experience, offering river rafting, hiking, and Jeep trips in the Rockies and the Sierra Nevada:

- Mission: We provide adventure travel with luxurious service.
- Target Market: Adventurous males and females, both singles and couples, ages 34 to 59, with sufficient discretionary income for our $750 to $3,700 trips.
- Goal: To grow our company substantially in 1997 through aggressive investment of 10% of sales in marketing.
- Purpose: To motivate people to request our video by calling a toll-free number.
- Message: We radiate excitement and conscientiousness, blended with proven expertise in the wilderness. We offer visually stirring river and backcountry trips, knowledgeable guides, and delicious food.
- Means: Marketing tools include a toll-free number, mailings, a Web site, printed collateral, a referral program, ads in select markets, PR articles, travel agency partnerships, trade shows, and free adventure-travel clinics.

178
IDEA

Package a Punch with Mini Newsletters

There's no time like the right time. **And the right time to reach customers is when they are most receptive.** Call them guided missives: Natural Ovens of Manitowoc, Wis., packed a one-page newsletter with every loaf of bread. Pete's Brewing, a microbrewer in Palo Alto, Calif., tucked a mini catalog into each six-pack.

The companies reached customers when they were most receptive. They also saved on postage and production. Natural Ovens printed its newsletter on the flip side of its bread label, which was folded lengthwise inside the loaf's plastic bag. Each week's issue included health tips, recipes, and letters from consumers. "Thousands of people called in response to the newsletter," reported Barbara Stitt, co-owner of the Natural Ovens bakery, which sold to 1,200 supermarkets. Increasing the label size to fit the newsletter raised costs only half a cent per loaf, but overall, printing the newsletter on the label saves her $1,000 an issue.

In a bookmark-size catalog that unfolds to 13 inches, Pete's Brewing told beer lovers about its sideline of T-shirts and mugs. Like other modern catalogs, "Wicked Ware" listed an 800 number, and in two years orders climbed to 1,200 a month. Pete's Brewing also passed out the profitable catalog at beer tastings. Talk about reaching customers when they're feeling good!

179
IDEA

A Cleaner Image

Industrial marketing material needn't be drop-dead dull. If a hazardous waste management company can make its operations look appealing, there's hope for every marketer. **Here's how several companies shaped their public image**:

In its latest brochure, Evergreen Environmental Group in Crestwood, Ky., traded mundane photos of microbes and test tubes for colorful back-to-nature illustrations. "The old brochure didn't say who we were," said Jerry McCandless, company president. He shifted focus to the end result—a cleaner environment—instead of the engineering means. Customers and prospects commented favorably on the new brochure, which featured an artist's rendition of a deer drinking from a stream.

Geoffrey Swett, marketing director in Tucson, Ariz., for Seattle-based Remediation Technologies (ReTec), discovered that stock photography could inexpensively customize marketing collateral for eight different niches. But, because any company can use the same photos, he also hired a seasoned environmental photographer to shoot a customer site. That photo made the cover of *Oil & Gas Journal* and remains a valuable reprint in ReTec's qualification pack. ReTec's sales grew 36% to $32 million during a flat industry sales period.

IDEA

Dish It Out on Disk

As the cost of printing rises, why not deliver a marketing piece that delivers real value to both company and customer? Computer disks may be your answer.

Jerry Weinstock, general manager of the bar-code printer division of Unimark Inc., in Overland Park, Kans., needed a marketing piece to present his division's capabilities and broaden Unimark's name recognition as a specialist in the field. To accomplish this without spending $15,000 on a brochure, he created the "Bar-Code Printer Desk Reference On Disk" using RoboHelp, a Windows help file-development tool by Blue Sky Software (800-793-0364). The desk reference includes printer comparisons, a glossary of terms, a guide to bar-code symbologies, and hyperlinks to bar-coding information on the Internet. It is distributed to prospects by mail and from Unimark's home page for no charge.

The project required a good dose of sweat equity, compiling source material from the bar-code industry trade association, employee-written articles, and other documents in the public domain. But the cost to distribute was minimal—$1.06 per disk for 2,500 pieces, and another 55 cents each for postage. According to Weinstock, this **high-tech marketing piece delivered identifiable value to prospects in his target marketplace** and was not likely to be thrown away. Over 4,000 desk references have been given to prospects, making Unimark's name and resources visible every day on a prospect's PC during the long sales cycle for bar-code printers.

Old-Fashioned Romance

If your business needs to appeal to a wider range of consumers, alter your marketing materials to play up romance or historic allure surrounding your business. David Nealley's business flourished when he tried this tactic with a seemingly unromantic product: garden tools.

For 130 years, Snow & Nealley in Bangor, Maine, sold axes to the logging industry, but imports started to undermine its profits. One day, during a tour of the company's facilities, customers "oohed" and "aahed" at the nine fire-spitting forges in the foundry. "Suddenly, I realized we had ambiance," said Nealley, "and we were undermarketing our product."

So Nealley **launched a complete marketing makeover**: He repackaged the company's tools, showing the fire-spitting forges in operation. The message was changed from a pitch about quality to a text evoking nostalgia. A hang-tag booklet that he created, about the care and use of hand tools, included a history of the company and stories about Daniel Boone and Teddy Roosevelt. Nealley also created a wrought-iron display for merchandising.

Customers took notice, and eventually, Snow & Nealley products were carried by more than 5,000 retailers, up from 500 six years earlier. "The packaging, displays, and booklet created romance," Nealley said. "Your products may have yesterday's quality, but you have to use today's aggressive marketing to convey that heritage to customers."

This Way to the Inn

For hotels, restaurants, and retailers, a busload of tourists can be a gold mine. But how do you attract the buses?

Bill Wollenhaupt and his wife owned the 28-room Horizon Inn, in Wilmington, Vt., and soon realized their volume was low, even though during the summer and foliage seasons they saw hundreds of tour buses pass through town. So, he called a few tour companies to find out how they decided where to lodge passengers. The tour agents said they spent hours making dozens of calls to find out numerous details about potential venues. Wollenhaupt hung up the phone and promptly got to work assembling the information for them.

He and his wife created a **28-page manual that described the inn**, quoted references from guests, and listed directions and details for many local attractions. They produced it on the computer, put copies in binders at minimal cost, and mailed them to 50 tour operators within a 400-mile radius.

"We made it easy for them," Wollenhaupt said, "and they've responded." Within one tour season the inn began to receive calls. Since introducing the handbook, Horizon's business grew 80%, most of it from tour groups.

Unique Business Cards

Business cards tell customers and products who you are, where you are, and how to contact you. But they can also tell what you do in a memorable way. With unique material or creative design, you can make your cards, and your business, stand out from the rest.

Instead of printing your cards on standard paper stock, explore alternative materials. For example, a paper bag salesman tucks his business cards into tiny paper bags. A Tyvek paper salesman prints his card on the indestructible material he sells—the material sells itself when he dares clients to try to tear his card.

You could also **use different designs, graphics, and business card shapes to represent your company** or products:

- A vice president of a bank makes his card look like a $5 bill folded in half. When he drops one on the ground, people race to pick them up.
- A watersports shop owner prints her card on translucent blue plastic. Not only is the card waterproof, but its background design evokes the feeling of water.
- American Sign and Indicator (the folks who make those time and temperature signs) have a calling card that displays the temperature. Tilt it slightly and the temperature changes to . . . the time.

Unique cards like these may cost a little extra, but they certainly leave an impression with customers and give them something to talk about.

184
IDEA

Quick to Print

Have a last-minute presentation? Need new marketing material overnight? Your computer is the miracle worker for producing **fast, professional, yet low-cost publicity** for your business.

Beliza Ann Furman put her computer to the test when her publicist gave her one week's notice for a book signing and discussion for her new book, *Younger Women—Older Men* (Barricade Books, 1995). Furman needed to quickly send press releases and brochures, on both her book and her public speaking services, to the media and event planners in the area.

First, she created a brochure in Microsoft Publisher and her press release in Microsoft Word. Next, she turned to her stockpile of matching brochure, letterhead, label, and envelope shells that she bought from PaperDirect (800-A-PAPERS), which could run through her laser printer. Within four hours Furman designed, printed, addressed, and stamped all her materials in time for the event. "As few as five years ago, this job would have taken over a week and involved a printing shop," she observes.

Furman's colorful mailing made an impression. She received a call back from every recipient, and her customer base grew 31%, mostly due to the target audience that received her do-it-yourself materials.

Cover All the Fax

Every day your company sends faxes, usually on cover sheets with empty space just begging to be used. So why not make faxes work twice as hard for you? **Redesign your fax cover sheets to include news about your company for customers and contacts**.

Regina Freize, marketing manager for Pacific Access, a leading technology systems integrator for the telecommunications industry in Rancho Cordova, Calif., finds that fax cover sheets are an excellent way to communicate information about her company to customers, suppliers, and vendors.

Freize designed her cover sheet in Adobe PageMaker, a page-layout program, and added a sidebar box, like those in magazine articles, that could be updated monthly. She used this box to announce new product updates, company achievements, special events, contests, surveys, facts, and any other information relating to the company that might be timely. "With the number of faxes we send out nationwide," Freize says, "this is the most cost-effective way to communicate corporate information—it's free!"

Freize believes that customers now have a much clearer picture of what the company does, and Pacific Access benefits from a stronger corporate identity and brand recognition.

186
IDEA

Book New Sales

During the rare moments of free time available while running their business, David and Martin Sher collaborated to **self-publish a book that became the ultimate sales tool for their company**, AmSher Financial Services, in Birmingham, Ala.

It took the brothers two years to write and publish *Championship Collections—How to Squeeze Blood from a Turnip*. When the book finally came off the press, David Sher sent copies to their local newspaper, the *Birmingham News*. An interview and photograph later, a color picture of the brothers and a favorable review of the book were featured on the front page of the Money section. Soon after, one of the city's largest bookstores wanted to buy copies for resale and asked the Shers to do a book signing. Trade associations, such as the American Collectors Association and State Bankers Association, featured articles about AmSher and their newsletters. The brothers started to receive invitations to speak at conferences and events all over the United States.

This was all very heady for the Shers, but more important, the book helped increase their financial services sales. Two years after the book was published, AmSher boasted 60% growth with no additional budget increase for advertising or marketing efforts. David Sher explains, "The book gave us credibility and did the selling for us. We can now say we wrote the book on collections."

X

"There's an assumption by many partners that no matter what happens to their businesses, they'll be partners forever."

—DAVID GIBBS, ESQ.
Peabody & Brown, Boston, Mass.

Networking in the Chamber

Your local Chamber of Commerce exists to help the growth of businesses in its area. For the price of dues, the Chamber is a great **resource for ideas, referrals, and potential customers**. Membership also entitles you to a free directory of Chamber members, and to purchase target mailing lists and other marketing resources. When you attend meetings and functions, you can build relationships with local VIPs and business owners. These relationships can be developed for sharing marketing ideas, referrals, and selling your product.

Joining certainly worked for Cheryl Spano, owner of Bianca's Biscuits & Baskets, a local and mail-order gift basket service located in Fitchburg, Mass. At her first Chamber function she met a person from a local hotel and began talking about Valentine's Day. She wound up making all the hotel's promotional baskets for Valentine's Day Weekend. The profit from the order well exceeded what she paid in annual dues.

188
IDEA

Power in Numbers

If you feel like a small fish in a sea of competition, consider joining a buying consortium to benefit from the power of numbers. Independent companies in industries, such as office supplies, furniture, and travel, in which small companies are threatened by large chains, combine forces to negotiate lower costs from suppliers and beef up their marketing efforts.

Kevin Melrose, owner of Village Travel in Scotts Valley, Calif., aligned his travel agency with Leisure Travel Group in Marina del Rey, Calif. Through this partnership, which includes thousands of agencies, Leisure obtains competitive prices and exclusive offers on travel packages, vacation extras that independent franchises can't offer, and an additional three to four points on commissions. "With an industry average of only 14% commission, the key to survival for us is volume and getting the best margins possible," says Melrose.

The group also negotiates packages that are advertised on full-color mailers, which each participating agency can purchase for only five cents each. By **pooling buying power and advertising resources** through this group, Village Travel has been able to stay in business since 1969.

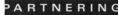

189
IDEA

Line Up Your Sponsors

Even a small company can launch a product with a national promotion, when **sponsors help share the costs for a media event**.

Few are doing it better than Suntex International, an Easton, Pa., game manufacturer. Founder Robert Sun promoted his new card game, "24," using a series of nationwide tournaments. The pilot tournament, which involved 3,000 elementary classrooms, proved so successful that Sun had no trouble winning the support of St. Paul Federal Bank as a sponsor.

Suntex hosted its first major tournament in Chicago, with four newspapers, five camera crews, and six radio stations covering the scene. The results were tangible and immediate: Toys "R" Us sold out of "24." Dominick's, a Chicago supermarket chain, sold 7,500 copies that Christmas season. Its competitor, Eagle Foods, sold 3,000. Soon manufacturers, banks, and the media began lining up to sponsor the "24 Challenge" in other cities.

In the end, Sun estimates the game and tournaments were covered in 15 top newspapers, with at least 100 mentions in print, radio, and television combined. "We've covered more than 60,000 classrooms at $10 a classroom, and most of that has been paid for by sponsors," proclaims Sun. "To get the same amount of publicity and product recognition, we'd have had to spend $3 million—strictly advertising."

Volunteer Sales Force

Nonprofit organizations have one thing most companies don't: enthusiastic volunteers willing to promote their organization. However, with the right partnership, and by agreeing to help raise money for such groups, you can **borrow these volunteers to promote your business** too.

Donating a percentage of receipts from a day's sales to an association encourages members and friends of members to buy from you. Or, allow clubs to sell memberships or non-competing products on your premises. Cheerleader car washes at gas stations employ this strategy.

Another way to leverage volunteers is to give products or services for a nonprofit to sell, raffle, or auction. For example, a local baker gives promoters of a local food festival 200 loaves of bread and allows them to keep whatever money they make from selling his bread. In return, the bakery gets exposure at the festival and is able to write off extra inventory for the cost of goods.

191
IDEA

Branding Together

If a humdrum product such as water can succeed under the Perrier brand name, Richard Hendler of Mamaroneck, N.Y., figured the same branding strategy could work for his Saxony Ice product.

However, Hendler couldn't afford to launch a widespread marketing campaign singlehandedly. Joining forces with another ice company, A.T. Reynolds & Sons in Kiamesha Lake, Hendler **formed a trade association** under the name Leisure Time Ice. The name conveyed the convenience of packaged ice, and the logo—a snow-capped mountain backed by blue sky and surrounded by green forests—suggested a clean and refreshing product that broke away from the traditional ice packaging mold. Hendler and Reynolds had the logo printed on bags, trucks, and company stationery for a total cost of $5,000.

Soon other ice manufacturers joined the association, widening its distribution area. During the next three years, the Leisure Time Ice association boasted 15 members and 60 trucks. It was selling about 13 million bags of ice annually, and association members' sales increased at least 10% a year. Hendler's own sales went from $458,000 to $1,700,000 in six years. His new business increased 40%, and his business with existing customers expanded 60%.

Like Perrier water, Leisure Time Ice may or may not have something special to offer that sets it apart from competitors. But by "branding together," a handful of small manufacturers have given their product national exposure and a touch of class.

Rolodex Party

Your friends and associates might recommend your business if they remember you and have an opportunity to do so. You might do the same for them. But instead of waiting for referral opportunities, you can make them happen immediately by **hosting a "Rolodex party"** with a friend, associate, or cooperative business owner.

Arnold Sanow, a consultant based in Vienna, Va., who hosts "Marketing Boot Camp" seminars across the country, used this mutually beneficial technique with an architect friend. Together, they spent an afternoon calling their clients with the express purpose of promoting each other.

Sanow called clients and asked them whether they were thinking of renovating their offices; if they were, he put the architect on the line. Then, the architect called associations of which he was a member and asked if they could use a speaker on marketing for any forthcoming meetings or conferences. In just four hours, the architect ended up with seven jobs and Sanow booked four speaking engagements.

193
IDEA

Points to the Group

Traditional frequent-buyer programs award "points" to customers every time they buy a product or service. But User Group Store puts a unique twist on this strategy. The $10-million Macintosh mail-order company in Soquel, Calif., **awards purchase points to the group or association its customers join**.

User Group Store sells discount hardware and software solely to current members of 2,300 Macintosh user groups (MUGs) in the nation. Since members of MUGs look to their group leaders for advice on what to buy and where to buy it, the group gets rewarded for the purchases its members make. MUG Leaders can redeem their points at any time to buy equipment and prizes for the group's use.

The points cost User Group Store approximately 1.5% of sales, but it's well worth it, says the store's president, Ray Kaupp. MUG leaders, in effect, become evangelists, recommending the mail-order store to their members through their meetings, newsletters, and Web pages. Several MUG officers released their membership databases so members could receive the monthly catalog, and as a result, the User Group Store's mailing list grew from 20,000 to 120,000 in less than six months. In its first year, members from 50 groups were active customers. Two years later, User Group Store boasts almost 100,000 customers who belong to hundreds of MUGs nationwide.

Good Neighbors Make Good Sellers

How do you sell a prospect equipment by catalog that he or she insists on test-driving? This was the question for Garden Way, the manufacturer of high-end Troy-Bilt power equipment that sold one-third of its products through its catalog and direct mail. However, many potential buyers who didn't have a Troy-Bilt retailer nearby wanted to test-drive the machines before they bought them. The solution: Garden Way put them in touch with a volunteer neighbor who owned one of the company's products.

Troy-Bilt owners apparently like to brag about their power equipment. The company recruited these customers into its Good Neighbor program at the time of their purchase by offering a special deal on the machines. Garden Way then listed them in the program's directory.

Of course, neither Garden Way nor any other company can control what a customer tells prospects about its products. So, before you recruit **customers as unofficial sales aides**, make sure they're huge fans of your products and services.

195
IDEA

PARTNERING

Bird-Dogging Your Prospects

Not enough cash to build a full-fledged sales organization and blanket the country? Consider **cultivating contacts in complementary industries** who, for a finder's fee, can open doors for your salespeople.

Laser Vision Centers, a provider of laser equipment and medical-marketing services in St. Louis, used just such a "bird-dog network" to extend its selling efforts. "We became a national company quicker than we would have otherwise," said CEO Jack Klobnak, who began using the referral system in 1987.

Independent sales reps for related products mentioned Laser Vision's name to their physicians and convinced them to meet with a full-time Laser Vision salesperson. If the meeting led to a sale, the independent sales rep received a finder's fee equal to 10% of Laser Vision's fee for services—less than what a full-time rep received, but enough to make it worth the effort.

"These fellows are in the neighborhood and know the people we want to sell to," said Klobnak, who estimated that his bird-dog network generated 20% to 25% of Laser Vision's leads. "If we got the opportunity to make the pitch," he added, "we made the sale about 40% of the time."

"I learned more from the
one restaurant that didn't
work than from all the ones
that were successes."

WOLFGANG PUCK
Restauranteur
Los Angeles, Calif.

196
IDEA

Cooperation with a Cause

If you're looking for more than a sales spike from your charity give-aways, why not **cohost your promotions with a compatible nonprofit organization**? You can develop a loyal customer base using long-term but very affordable campaigns.

Razcal Corp. of Wayland, Mass., needed its raspberry-lime soda to be clearly identified by the teen market. So, the company teamed up with Mothers Against Drunk Driving (MADD). Not only does MADD target teens, it also addresses the issue of beverage consumption.

For years MADD had tried to get schools to participate in a poster contest with an anti-drinking theme, but received a lackluster response. Razcal paid for and executed a slick direct-mail campaign for the poster contest, targeting 4,000 high schools in New England. The results were dramatic: three thousand students, representing 500 schools, participated in the contest. Razcal honored the winners at several sock hops, and picked up the costs for prizes, music, and plenty of Razcal soda.

All told, the mailers, poster kits, T-shirts and other prizes cost Razcal approximately $25,000. In addition, the company gave away about 100,000 cans of soda—and it was worth it. Razcal's overall sales doubled from 250,000 cases to 500,000 in one year. In areas where schools joined the campaign, sales doubled and even tripled for the entire year. In addition, supermarkets waived slotting fees and even provided point-of-purchase displays to ally themselves with the MADD-Razcal anti-drinking effort.

Service Swap

Getting a business off the ground may be the biggest hurdle for many entrepreneurs, but finding customers places a close second. Diaper Dan, a start-up diaper service in West Haven, Conn., had thousands of Chinese diapers, a driver, and a 12-foot van. Founder Dan Gold's greatest challenge was to find his market.

Gold took aim at what the business world calls "influencers" to do some selling for him—through **offering free service, products, and promotion in exchange for referrals**. His first targets were midwives, Lamaze teachers, and nurses, all of whom gave lessons on diapering as part of their instruction to new mothers. Gold searched for these influencers at 12 area hospitals and received a positive response.

Diaper Dan had what they needed: comprehensive educational tools ("ed packs") free of charge. The kits included a diapering instruction manual, a company brochure, and a dozen luxurious Chinese diapers stamped with Diaper Dan's name.

Gold also approached the regional La Leche League, an organization that promotes breast-feeding, and volunteered to underwrite the cost of its telephone directories. He visited stores that carried children's goods and asked them to display his business cards and brochures in exchange for distributing their coupons to his customers.

Gold's legwork quickly paid off. Just four months after its formal launch, Diaper Dan's customer base weighed in at 350 and was growing exponentially. Referrals came from referrals. By the end of the first year, Gold had over 1,500 customers, four times his projection.

198
IDEA

Mutual Recommendation Society

Take a tip from the world of fast-food and **reduce your marketing costs by getting your retail partners to sell for you**. Every time you order a burger at a fast-food restaurant, the teenager behind the counter asks: "Want some fries with that?" That question boosts the amount of the average purchase, and reduces the potato suppliers' marketing costs by selling the fries for them.

Gus Blythe used this strategy at SecondWind, his shoe-care company in Paso Robles, Calif. Shoe manufacturers and retailers did a good part of his selling for him. He marketed to them, and they, in turn, took his message to hundreds of thousands of potential customers. If a shoe company gave SecondWind an endorsement, he put pictures of their sneakers on his shoe-care product.

Blythe maintained that if the customer took care of shoes with his product, they would be worn more than other shoes, and therefore the customer would buy a new pair sooner. As an extra inducement, he encouraged manufacturers to put his address on their shoe tags so consumers could contact him to learn about shoe care. The manufacturers bought his arguments. Out of the 10 largest sneaker companies, only Reebok, Nike, and Adidas didn't recommend SecondWind.

199
IDEA

A Name That Launches Sales

In today's market, it takes millions of dollars and time to build a nationally-known brand name and succeed in the mass market. If you don't have the money and don't want to wait, **obtain a license so you can sell your products under an already-established brand name**.

Helen of Troy Corp., a hair-dryer manufacturer in El Paso, Texas, auditioned against other companies for a license from Vidal Sassoon. While the competition was fierce, Helen of Troy offered the best deal: $100,000 upon signing, plus 10% of sales, compared with the standard 6% royalty.

Founder Gerry Rubin would have preferred the growth to come from products with his company's name, but that just wasn't going to happen. "Sure, it was a lot of money," says Rubin, "but what choice did we have? We needed the name." They got it. And the name got them shelf space. Three years later, Helen of Troy's revenues jumped by two-thirds, to nearly $68 million. Earnings nearly tripled.

200 IDEA

Flowering Partnership with Nonprofits

Partnering with a nonprofit organization is not only admirable, it can bring you new customers at a lower cost than traditional methods of promotion. That's what happened when Flowers Direct, a floral-ordering service in Tampa, formed an **"affinity partnership"** with Paralyzed Veterans of America (PVA), a group that seeks to ease the wounds of war.

Flowers Direct, which fielded orders to top-rated florists across the country, set up an exclusive toll-free number through which the PVA automatically received a $5 contribution for every order at no additional cost to the customer. The company also donated floral arrangements for PVA events. The PVA, in turn, promoted Flowers Direct among its members and donors, advertised the partnership in *PN/Paraplegia News and Dateline* (a PVA employee magazine), and distributed Flowers Direct collateral at expositions and other gatherings.

Patty Grenhart, vice president of marketing at Flowers Direct, said the collaborative effort was gratifying. The company booked thousands of floral gift orders generated by the partnership. PVA received many donations and increased national advertising, and both organizations benefited from bouquets of goodwill.

XI

"The moment you make
a mistake in pricing, you're
eating into your reputation
or your profits."

KATHARINE PAINE
founder of the Delahaye Group,
Hampton Falls, N.H.

IDEA

Giveaways for Good Customers

How do you reward customers for buying more? **Discounts and favorable terms on high-volume purchases are a start**. Another way to encourage customers to spend more is to give them a gift from your excess inventory when their purchase amount reaches a specified figure.

Barb Todd, owner of a $21-million mail-order business in Portland, Ore., knows it works. Each time a customer spends $250 or more on a single order from her Good Catalog, she sends a gift. Although it's called the "Really Outrageous Gift Program," her system is hardly excessive, because she selects her gifts from leftover inventory or product samples, and ships them with a personalized letter. The average gift has a $75 retail value, yet it is really worth about $15 at the warehouse sale where it would otherwise be sold. Todd is glad to give up a little something to encourage large sales. "It costs me more money to process ten $25 orders," she says.

According to Todd, the freebie's effect is dramatic. Within a few months of starting the program, the gift recipients' response rates to mailings rose from 5% to 25%, while the amount of their average purchases increased from $100 to $300.

Negotiate with Pricing Guidelines

When an industry changes so much that companies can't price products or services the way they used to, they may need a new philosophy: **provide pricing guidelines, not inflexible rules**. Patty DeDominic, CEO of $19-million PDQ Personnel Services, in Los Angeles, used to charge a recruitment fee for permanent employees, and charge by the hour for temporary placements. Today, she is forced to negotiate each contract individually to keep from losing business.

Her 13 employees who price contracts know that costs are about 30% above direct labor, so they add a markup of 30% (for breakeven) to 80%, depending on who the client is, the length of the assignment, and the risk factors. Employees are informed of project profitability and receive rewards for good pricing decisions. Since the new policy was instituted, PDQ's profit-sharing contribution has doubled.

Profit-Sharing Payment

If a customer is strapped for cash, one way to overcome objections to your prices is to negotiate profit-sharing deals rather than fee-for-service payments.

Stan Brannan, chairman of the board for Brite Voice Systems, a voice-processing services company in Wichita, Kan., went this route during an industry downturn. He looked for situations in which a customer was going to use his equipment to generate new business, then **offered to take a cut rather than a one-time fee**. Individual contracts detailed "shared deductible expenses" such as the cost of installing additional telephone lines. Net revenue was then split equally between both partners.

Thanks in part to Brannan's scheme, Brite Voice's revenues skyrocketed from $35 million to $47 million in just one year, with one-third of its business from profit-sharing contracts.

204
IDEA

Underpricing Fiasco

You want customers to think they're getting a good deal, but there's no point in selling yourself short. If you underprice yourself, customers might think you're worthless, and you could choke your company's profits. **One way to determine the best price point: conduct a direct-mail campaign that tests different offers**.

When Approach Software, in Redwood City, Calif., launched its first product, it wanted to offer a low introductory price to persuade users to try its database software program. Jaleh Bisharat, Approach's marketing director, interviewed prospects and got confirmation that the $149 price point she was considering was reasonable. Then, to be sure, she sent out 50,000 direct-mail offers with price points of $99, $129, and $149. The mailing provided the "statistical proof" Bisharat needed when almost equal sales came in at $149 and $129. The company then tested a $199 price, but that "crossed a threshold of what people would spend to try a new product through the mail," said CEO Kevin Harvey.

The low initial price did its job. One month after the product began shipping, Approach landed on industry bestseller lists. Three months later, the company raised the suggested retail price to $399 ($279 street price) and the product remained a top seller.

205
IDEA

Managing Expectations

Pricing a new service is tricky because it's hard to project the cost of intangibles—for example, how often customers will call for support or need features not in the contract. "It's not like buying a car, where you can see all the extras," said Alan Shusterman, CEO of CMG Health, a company in Owings Mills, Md., that packages mental-health care for insurance agencies and health maintenance organizations.

Having underpriced once or twice, **he began focusing on understanding customers' expectations**. For CMG, that meant helping customers distinguish a basic benefits package from one with the "extras" (more hospitals, big-name doctors, more information on treatment usage).

"We got customers to explain exactly what their assumptions were," said Shusterman. To help customers define their needs, CMG's salespeople brought in regional service administrators—who worked closely with the care providers—to explain the specifics of each package. CMG got the customer to sign off on what was discussed, and allowed later renegotiation if necessary.

CMG's approach lengthened the sales cycle, but only one of the company's 30 clients cancelled a contract on the basis of service.

206
IDEA

Low-Price Licensing

Sometimes tough markets call for new pricing models. Marcel Mendoza, CEO of Edutech, a software distributor in Monterey, Calif., has doubled her sales each year with innovative pricing.

To overcome resistance in the educational market, Mendoza adapted a pricing model that colleges were familiar with: textbooks. Educators couldn't fathom buying one of the $500 word-processing programs Edutech distributes. But they warmed to the idea of software priced about the same as a calculus text. "Schools were crying for a good price," says Mendoza. So, she offered each school **a site license based on volume**.

Working with the college, Edutech projects how many students and faculty members will buy the software, plus how many copies will be used in the campus computing center. The minimum license sold is for 25 users. "It's like having collective individual buyers," says Mendoza.

Once the school buys the license, students can purchase software from the college bookstore for an average price of $35 to $75. Mendoza can pass on 90% discounts because her own costs are reduced—the school receives one set of disks and must make its own copies of the software. Edutech provides the manuals, minus the boxes.

Since her first experiment, Mendoza has persuaded more software vendors for whom she acts as a distributor to adopt her strategy. She now moves $10 million in software for 15 vendors, about 35% of it through site licensing.

207
IDEA

Brand Yourself and Your Service

Dave Voracek, a marketing consultant in Arlington, Va., made his services easier for clients to buy and increased his consulting sales by **branding himself and packaging one of his services as a unique, low-cost bundle**.

Voracek offered a wide range of marketing tools on an hourly basis, but most clients needed a basic brochure, or an improvement on the one they already had. So, Voracek packaged a 12-point brochure check-up service and report for $85. Once clients hired him for this small job, he built a relationship with them that led to selling his other services.

To play up his service, Voracek bought a white lab coat and a stethoscope and wore them to networking events where he introduced himself as the "Brochure Doctor." When people approached him to ask, "What kind of doctor are you?" He replied, "I fix sick brochures that need an injection of creativity.

"I've built a higher business profile in the past four years than I had in the previous 10 years as just the guy-in-a-blue-suit marketing consultant," Voracek said.

208
IDEA

Price by the Slice

Some customers require more service than others, but most companies charge everyone the same amount. That didn't make a lot of sense to David and Linda West of San Luis Sourdough Company. They said **folks should pay for what they get**—so the couple used this philosophy to set prices, and passed the cost of service on to their customers.

The Wests, owners of the San Luis Obispo, Calif., bakery, priced their products according to how much service their customers—area supermarkets and small specialty-food stores—required.

If a supermarket was satisfied with a bread drop-off at the back door, the wholesale price for this Level 1 service was 97 cents a loaf. If the store wanted to return day-old bread for full credit (Level 2), the cost was $1.02 a loaf. And if the store wanted the company to put the bread on the shelf, price it with a bar-code label on each bag and another on the shelf, and accept returns (Level 3), the price climbed to $1.05.

Those prices weren't arbitrary; instead of eating the 5 cents or 8 cents a loaf it would cost to give additional service, the Wests made their customers pay for it. They reduced their costs and boosted their profits. Pretax margins at San Luis Sourdough top 10%.

Better Business Bundling

Bundling products together can help move regularly-priced products when sales go soft—especially when the market for the product is weak to begin with.

That's what Chuck Sussman found when he was running Pretty Neat Industries, in Pompano Beach, Fla., and sales of his cosmetics-organizer began to fall off. He didn't want to reduce prices, because that probably wouldn't have generated enough new sales to make up for the loss in profitability per sales unit.

"I was planning to introduce a new version of the organizer at about half the regular price," recalls Sussman. "Instead, I priced the cheaper model at 10% off full price, shrink-wrapped the old and new products into one package, and stuck on a Day-Glo banner that said 'Free $4 value with this purchase!' "

Not only were Sussman's margins higher on the combination pack than they would have been if he had sold the products separately, but the package sold like hotcakes. "Customers kept the expensive product and gave the inexpensive one as a gift," Sussman says. "And, of course, we wound up increasing our margins, not cutting them, which is what would have happened if we'd cut prices."

XII

"Different is what sells. Our customers want to go into a place of business that's different. They want to shop at stores that stock diverse merchandise and have diverse promotions. It's the key to not only staying ahead, but staying in business: have different types of merchandise, and use different types of promotions. By doing things differently, people will come to you."

RICK SEGEL
retail consultant and founder of
Rick Segel and Associates, Burlington, Mass.

210
IDEA

No Fortune, Just Fame

Contests can greatly increase responses to ads, surveys, and feedback requests—especially when a big prize is offered. But, if your budget won't tolerate high-ticket items in the five-figure range, consider alternative rewards, such as fame and media exposure.

Pro-Mark, a $10-million drumstick maker in Houston, ran a contest appealing to the egos of aspiring drummers. It printed a simple black-and-white ad in *Modern Drummer* (the industry's leading magazine) asking readers to nominate themselves as the "Not Yet Famous Drummer," and promised to feature the winner in subsequent Pro-Mark ads.

Five thousand readers sent in photos of themselves and filled out a survey card indicating which drumsticks, bands, and music styles they preferred, doubling the size of Pro-Mark's database. **The company used this contest response information to build a mailing list**, create better products, and target future ads. "Pro-Mark's customer base is made up of countless thousands of nameless drummers," says Herb Brochstein, founder of Pro-Mark. "Now, more of them are likely to remember the Pro-Mark name."

211
IDEA

This Call Brought to You by...

Imagine thousands of people picking up their telephones and hearing a marketing message from your company. It's possible with **prepaid phone cards**.

When a Chicago man opened his Father's Day gift box of pasta sauce, he found among the goodies a telecard giving him 10 free minutes of long-distance calling time. Dialing in for the free time, he heard this message: "Happy Father's Day from Uncle Dave's and Marshall Fields, and thank you for shopping." The telecard was prepared by SmarTel for Uncle Dave's Kitchen, a $3-million operation in South Londonderry, Vt., as a value-added incentive for stores to carry its gift baskets of pasta sauces and condiments.

Uncle Dave's CEO, David Lyons, spent $1,625 to design and produce his first batch of customized cards. When a Fourth of July promotion rolled around, Lyons discovered he could update his card's messages electronically. Overall, he spent $17,625 for the cards and achieved his goal of getting into the gift market business.

212 IDEA

Attention, Shoppers!

If it works for Kmart, why can't it work for you? You can **use your store's public address system** to announce the arrival of new products, sales, or special events. You may even be able to automate the process with a recording or by tuning in to a satellite broadcast.

John Clarke, president of a two-store grocery business in Mitchell, S.D., says that when it comes to technology, he's right up there with the big boys. County Fair Food Stores pays $30 a month for a satellite system that receives broadcasts from manufacturers—including commercial and discount information specifically designed for products sold in their stores—then plays them over the store speakers. The broadcasts help push items in the stores that otherwise might not move off the shelves fast enough. And the system saves time and money because Clarke's employees don't have to produce or announce the pre-recorded broadcasts.

213
IDEA

By Invitation Only

Make your high-volume customers, influencers, and VIPs feel special by **opening your store for an invitation-only sales event** on a day you are normally closed. Host the event with catered food, prepare discount items, and provide opportunities for your invitees to get to know each other.

The Red Balloon, a children's book store in St. Paul, Minn., opens its doors for a party on Labor Day. As customers and influencers for their books, teachers have the store to themselves. Every book is on sale for that day only. The special customers are served donut holes, juice, and coffee. They can take away publisher's posters and book covers to decorate their classrooms. At the end of the party, a few of the latest books are raffled off as door prizes. The event allows teachers to socialize and share their favorite book choices with each other.

Approximately 250 teachers attend The Red Balloon's annual Teacher's Sale, and most purchase books before they leave. "We don't track this, but we find other educators and parents come to our store by recommendation from these teachers," says manager Michele Poire.

214
IDEA

Giveaways in Costume

Costumed characters handing out product samples get customers' attention and create a memorable exchange. A stunt like this could also lead to a groundswell of publicity and word-of-mouth advertising.

Ken Myers, co-founder of Smartfood, did it when he was first trying to promote his snack popcorn that came in a unique, resealable bag. "Every time we could get Smartfood into someone's mouth, we knew they would like the taste experience and tell others," he recalls.

Myers hired people to dress in giant popcorn bags to ski down New England ski slopes. **Samples were given out to curious people passing by** the "skiing bags." Another time, during a concert of controversial rap group 2 Live Crew, whose hit song was "Me So Horny," Smartfood's popcorn-bag mascots stood outside the concert and sang their own song: "Me So Corny." The media covered the rapping popcorn bags, and again, Smartfood popcorn made the rounds.

215
IDEA

High-Flying Sales Incentives

Companies that offer **products or services already used and valued by your target market** may provide you with a sales incentive that's cost-effective, interests your customers, and matches your company image.

Tod Meier, president of Roger Meier Cadillac in Dallas, was looking for an incentive to draw customers to his dealership and induce them to buy. However, his discerning clientele did not identify well with price gimmicks, rebates, and cheap product giveaways. Then Meier realized most of his customers flew on Dallas-based American Airlines and were members of the AAdvantage frequent-flyer program. He made a few calls to the airline, and found out he could purchase award miles for 2 cents per mile, plus a service charge. He sent a mailer to local luxury car owners and placed newspaper ads offering 500 airline miles for test-driving a Cadillac and 10,000 miles for buying one.

With a cost of only $200 per car sold, Meier spent less than the price of most dealership incentive strategies. After ringing up a 50% increase in business from the previous year, he expanded his frequent-flyer miles incentive to his Infiniti and Oldsmobile dealerships, service departments, and used-car sales.

216
IDEA

Customer Equity in a Good Idea

Giving up equity is a dreadful thought for many company founders, but not for Andrew Martin. He gave away stock in his company to new customers—which was central to his growth strategy.

Martin, cofounder of Good Idea Foods, a start-up snack-food marketer based in Chelsea, Mass., thought that **giving away stock would help build a loyal following for his products**. He set aside 10% of the company, or 400,000 shares, for the public. Good Idea's bags of snack food products trumpeted the offer: "Free Share of Stock . . . See Details on Back." For a limited time, anyone could send up to 10 self-addressed, stamped envelopes to the address printed on the bag and receive a free share of stock for each envelope.

Whether or not stockholders would buy Good Idea products, the company was responsible for keeping track of as many as 400,000 of them. Martin focused on these shareholders with the hopes that they would become loyal consumers who would build the company's revenues.

217
IDEA

Soft Sell

A new customer walks into your store, browses around, and then says, "I'll think about it and come back later." But folks like that never do. They go down the street to the competitor to see what else is available and compare prices. Bruce Wisman, vice-president of a retail appliance store in Fort Wayne, Ind., wanted his store to be the last one customers stopped at before going home. He needed to **devise a plan to discourage browsers from shopping at other appliance stores**.

At the suggestion of Jeff Slutsky, author of *Streetfighters Marketing*, Wisman filled a freezer with gallons of ice cream and, just before customers left the store, he handed each one a free carton.

Not only did the customers' hearts melt at Wisman's generosity, so did the ice cream, and people hurried home to get it into the freezer. That put an end to comparison shopping for the day and left Wisman's appliances on his customers' minds.

 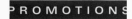
"The market is not an invention
of capitalism. It has existed
for centuries. It is an invention
of civilization."

MIKHAIL GORBACHEV
June 8, 1990

Tee-off with Sponsorship Tournaments

There are 25 million golfers; some should be selling for me, thought Corky Newcomb, founder of C.N. Is Believing (CNIB), in Wolfeboro Falls, N.H.

Back in 1989, retailers didn't believe anyone played golf at night, and wouldn't stock the company's Nitelite golf ball, the latest of its glow-in-the-dark sporting goods. Newcomb needed to spread the word where it counted—on the golf course. He aimed a campaign at amateur golfers: Persuade your club to sponsor its first Nitelite tournament and get a $100 reward.

Newcomb promoted the offer through half-page ads in 10 golf magazines, which cost him about $150,000 a year, roughly 60% of his ad budget. The **grass-roots promotion** landed CNIB accounts with 4,700 clubs which eventually grew to 14,000 clubs as regular customers. Some 95,000 Nitelite tournaments have been held in 59 countries; exports grew to more than 17% of sales. Tournament sales (balls, tees, putters, hats, mugs, and light sticks to illuminate the course) brought in 55% of CNIB's total revenues. Plus, the tournaments helped Newcomb sell to specialty golf shops and mass merchants in all 50 states.

219
IDEA

Loss-Leader Coupon

Joe Blise, owner of a Mail Boxes Etc. franchise in Green Bay, Wis., doesn't publish a discount good for any purchase in his store or off his most profitable items. Instead, he offers discounts only on photocopies, one of his most popular services.

"I don't make any money on four-cent photocopying," says Blise. His coupon does what it needs to—bring people into the store so he can **show customers the other non-discounted and profitable services** he provides. While customers wait for their copies, Blise can talk to customers or give them a chance to browse through the store and discover his shipping and mailing services. On one occasion, Blise turned a 40-cent copy sale into $200 of monthly business.

"We will never try to develop
a strategy that wins on
price. There is nothing unique
about pricing."

JOSH S. WESTON
Chairman and CEO of
Automatic Data Processing, Inc.

It Pays to Be Loyal

Chances are your company could benefit from increased customer loyalty. So, why not borrow a tried and true customer-loyalty gimmick? That's what Dallas-based One Hour Delivery Service (OHDS) did when it adapted the airline industry's frequent flyer concept to their courier business.

Like the plans it mimics, OHDS's **frequent-caller program** rewards customers that use its service—mainly decision-making secretaries, mail clerks, and receptionists. Customers accrue one point for each delivery, except for downtown deliveries, which get only one-tenth of a point. Statements of point balances are sent three times a year, along with information about popular rewards such as chocolates and a dozen roses.

"The program continues to be extremely popular and the customer loyalty that it generates makes it well worthwhile," reports Regina McLean, owner of the courier business.

It Feels Good to Belong

If Frank Perdue could create a brand image for chicken, Jack C. Davis figured he could do the same for title insurance services. Davis, regional manager for First American Title Insurance in St. Louis, **differentiated his business and developed branding for an intangible product** by turning his office into a club and his clients into members.

Davis first sent two anonymous postcards to his prospective customers—local real estate agents. The first said, "The Eagle Is Coming!" The second said, "The Eagle Is Coming Soon!" The third mailing, packaged in an envelope, said, "The Eagle Has Arrived!" Inside, a brochure announced First American Title's Silver Eagle Service Club and listed services and benefits that were "exclusive" to members. Also accompanying the brochure was a letter from Davis and a reply card (postage required) that could be sent in for more information.

Was the Silver Eagle Service Club exclusive? No. Any agent who asked could join it. "Asking to join the club," says Davis, "was the same thing as asking to be my client." Did members receive special benefits or incentives? No, nothing more than they should have expected from any company handling real-estate closings. "It was mostly what we were doing before," says Davis, "but we packaged the services and gave them a name."

From the 9,000 names to whom Davis initially mailed, he signed up 380 new agents, and the St. Louis First American office generated as much business during the first five months of the club's existence as in the first nine months of the previous year.

"The secret is to know your customer. Segment your target as tightly as possible. Determine exactly who your customers are, both demographically and psychographically. Match your customer with your medium. Choose only those media that reach your potential customers, and no others. Reaching anyone else is waste."

ROBERT GREDE
author of *Naked Marketing, the Bare Essentials*
(Prentice Hall, 1997)

222
IDEA

I'll Guarantee Anything

Long the province of late-night TV pitchmen, the **money-back guarantee** shows up in surprising places.

G.T. Rapp, a Seattle ad agency, began offering a guaranteed goals program. Owner Gregg Rapp met with clients to establish goals and methods to measure them, whether it was boosting a direct-mail response rate or increasing sales. If the goal went unmet, Rapp refunded account service fees, which usually represented 25% of the ad project.

Rapp said his $1-million firm had little choice but to offer guarantees. "So many of our clients came to us with a bad taste in their mouths after working with large agencies and seeing no results. It was the only way to prove we were different."

223
IDEA

Coupon for Their Name

A coupon doesn't have to just offer a discount—use it to get important customer information too.

After spending time telling a customer about the benefits of your product line, you don't want him or her to walk out before you get a name and phone number. Barry Fribush, founder of Bubbling Bath Spa & Tub Works in Rockville, Md., made sure that didn't happen—he gave out coupons for $125 worth of merchandise while making the sales pitch. Fribush's salespeople told prospects that because this was a special offer, the company needed to **track every coupon**, and get their name, address, and phone number on the spot. The coupons were redeemable for a chemical kit, pillows, and extra filter cartridges.

What if the customer balked? "We said, 'that's perfectly okay, but we need the coupon back,'" noted Fribush. In the seven years he gave out coupons, maybe a handful of prospects gave them back. Once he had their names, he followed up with phone calls and placed them on his mailing lists.

224

IDEA

Give and You Shall Receive

To turn first-time skiers and equipment buyers into lifetime customers, Leslie B. Otten, president of Sunday River Skiway in Bethel, Maine, **gave products away to first-time customers**, not once but four times.

Novices who wanted to learn how to ski at Sunday River paid $33 for a lesson, which included free equipment (worth $18) and a free lift ticket (worth $33). New skiers could also sign up for two additional lessons, with the same benefits. Students who completed all three lessons got a coupon for a fourth day of free skiing. And to make that and subsequent visits even more attractive, Otten sold students skis, boots, and poles at cost.

"While we weren't making any money on this guaranteed-learn-to-ski program," said Otten, "we weren't losing any money, either." It was good business. Sunday River Skiway came out way ahead on the long-term benefits. Before the program, only 20% of Sunday River's first-time customers returned. After the program launched, more than 75% revisited the ski area. Repeat visits were a major reason Sunday River's pretax income increased about fourfold, to $4 million a year.

REAL WORLD

"Don't tell people how to do things. Tell them what to do and let them surprise you with their results."

GEORGE S. PATTON, JR.
military general and diplomat

Make Customers Say Cheese

Most people like to have their picture taken. It makes them feel important. So **turn photo opportunities into quality promotion pieces** for your business.

At Eriez Magnetics, a manufacturer of magnetic laboratory and metal detection equipment, the receptionist lined up visiting customers underneath a sign with the company trademark on it and snapped their picture. "It's just our way of saying thank you," said Chet Giermak, president and CEO. "We're complimented that you would come all the way to Erie, Pa., just to see us."

The photos also served a practical purpose. Giermak sent them to visitors with a cover letter reminding them of the reason for the visit and the people with whom they met. He slipped the photo into a cardboard frame with the company's mission statement on the back. It only took a minute to dictate the letter, and each complete package, including the stamp, cost $2. Upon receipt, several potential customers made a second sales appointment.

226
IDEA

Reward for Spreading the Word

If you can reward customers for being customers, you can also reward them for sending you the names of their friends.

California Cosmetics, in Chatsworth, Calif., sold makeup, skin-care products, and inexpensive knockoffs of well-known perfumes such as Opium, Passion, and Obsession. President Robert Sidell promised his mail-order customers the knockoff of their choice for free if they would **supply him with the names of three people who might like his cosmetics**.

About 20% of his customers took him up on the offer, and for every three new names he got, one placed an order. In the direct-mail business, a 33% conversion rate was unheard of. If three people out of 100 who get your catalog became customers, you were a superstar.

But Sidell said his results weren't surprising. "First, we got qualified leads. The people recommending us usually believed that their friends would like our products. Second, they generally told their friends why they liked doing business with us. That made it easier to convert them."

227
IDEA

A Place to Race

Looking for new ways to boost sales? Turn your store over to your customers for a day.

Bob Wilke, vice president of HobbyTown U.S.A. and operator of four of its franchises, feeds his customers' passion by **providing them with an avenue to use and enjoy his products**. His most valuable business asset is the enthusiasm young customers have for his radio-control cars and other hobby-related products.

Each Saturday, Wilke, of Lincoln, Nebr., ropes off a section of his parking lot to host a one-tenth-scale car race for his young customers. More than 20 kids pay a nominal fee to race around the track against their friends. The races last almost all day, and the winner of the final heat receives free products or a gift certificate from Wilke's store.

The event draws people in from around the strip mall, and increases foot traffic near the store. Wilke reports a 30% increase in sales on car parts and accessories on race days, and every week HobbyTown sets up at least one new car owner. The race attracts car racers and friends who are new to the hobby, and encourages existing customers to remain loyal to the store. Entry fees make the event a break-even tactic, but increased annual sales make it a profitable strategy. By helping customers put their purchases into action, HobbyTown has experienced a 30% annual increase in sales.

228
IDEA

Gains at Every Level

With just a single promotion, **a manufacturer can drive customers to dealers** and encourage dealers to advocate its products instead of the competitors'. The secret: plan a promotion from which everybody has something to gain.

A Southern California manufacturer of premium fly-fishing reels ranging in price from $450 and up took its customers' order information, segmented addresses into zip code regions, and gave those names to dealers in those areas. The dealers sent out a "free test drive" letter—created by the manufacturer—inviting these people to try the reels with a promise of a gift just for coming in, no strings attached. (The reel manufacturer supplied the inexpensive gift to the dealers at cost.) Dealers who sold 10 reels and sent the letters and receipts back to the manufacturer would receive a free reel to demonstrate, give away, or sell.

The strategy turned out to be a win-win-win situation. Customers got a great reel and a free gift. When letter recipients came in, the dealers had an incentive to fully demonstrate and sell the manufacturer's reels. Since the letters were sent back, the manufacturer was able to build a valuable database of new reel owners who respond to direct mail. And even if recipients of the free gift didn't buy the reel, dealers brought new customers into their store. As for the numbers, approximately 50,000 letters sent out by 175 dealers brought in 5,000 new customers and sold 2,900 reels—a whopping 10% return and 58% sales response.

229
IDEA

Impressions in the End Zone

Many companies, like Medi-Centre, a medication supply service in Lansing, Mich., are realizing that it pays **to pitch to the customers' customers**.

At nursing homes and adult fostercare facilities, nurses are the decision makers in choosing medication supply services. But Medi-Centre's Beth Kinerk decided to bypass nurses and instead target her customers' customers—the resident seniors—to land new contracts.

Before a facility signed anything, Kinerk would host a "Family Night" for patients and their families to show them how their medication would be administered. She filled Medi-Centre's color-coded "punch packs" with colorful chocolate candies. That gave the nurses a clear idea of how the medications were prepackaged, while the seniors got a snack and a keepsake with Medi-Centre's name, address, and phone number on it. The seniors loved it, and what made them happy made the nurses happy.

Kinerk's bottom-up strategy succeeded beyond her expectations. Medi-Centre grew 1,108% per year on average since Kinerk's employment with the company. The company now services 5,000 beds—up from 100 three years ago.

230
IDEA

Paid Evangelists

Arm your customers with business cards, certificates, or even a verbal understanding, and they'll be motivated to tell their friends—and even total strangers—to purchase from you, if you make it worth their while.

At Indy Lube, customers who send friends to any shop in the quick-lube chain receive a $10 certificate toward their next oil change. It's a way to thank customers who take the time to fill out an Indy Lube **referral card** and give it to a friend. The new customer uses the card to get $5 off the first oil change.

Each time Indy Lube runs a contest among its 28 locations for the most customer referrals in a month, CEO Jim Yates says it redeems as many as 50 referral cards per store.

XIII

"You can get free press by doing outrageous things. One time a couple of local morning deejays were talking about our yogurt, and one told the other on the air that he'd rather eat camel manure than yogurt. We heard about it, brought him a quart of fresh camel manure on air, and got about 3 months of play after he reluctantly agreed that the yogurt tasted better."

GARY HIRSHBERG
founder of Stonyfield Farm Yogurt,
Wilton, N.H.

231
IDEA

Sincere Apologies

Who said nice folks finish last? Iris Harrell of Menlo Park, Calif., would say that's nonsense, since 65% of her $3.2-million remodeling company's revenues last year came from previous customers and referrals.

Harrell spends 70% of her marketing budget on **low-cost goodwill efforts that encourage repeat business** and generate referrals. For example, during each project involving kitchen remodeling, she sends customers a handwritten note apologizing for the inconvenience, and includes a gift certificate for dinner. She budgets about $1,500 a year for gift certificates to local restaurants.

Harrell also remembers the potential inconvenience to neighbors. "It's really about creating a positive presence in the community," she says. "Pardon Our Dust" letters are sent to everyone who lives near one of her construction sites. Each letter asks the neighbor to call if there are any noise, trash, or parking problems.

Recently, three homeowners who lived on the same street did call. Instead of complaining, they asked Harrell to bid on their own remodeling projects. All three had been referred to her by their neighbors—four past customers of Harrell's—and her entire marketing budget is only 1% of sales.

232
IDEA

Enter Contests, Win Big

Every company craves free publicity. And what better way to get it than by earning an award? Ruppert Landscape of Ashton, Md., made a practice of entering contests for which its landscape work would have a fighting chance. Past achievements range from a City of Alexandria Beautification Award to an American Association of Nurserymen Award hosted by the White House.

Ruppert put considerable time, materials, and training into competing for awards. Each year it spent $7,000, about 6% of the public-relations budget, solely on entry fees and award banquets. What were the payoffs? As a result of press releases issued by Ruppert and the award giver, each year the company **received coverage in major magazines and newspapers**. Also, both customers and employees could brag about their achievements. Morale went up and so did sales—to $22 million.

233
IDEA

Publish or Perish

If you have expertise or a story to share, you can get free exposure by **writing an article for your industry's trade magazines**. Many publications accept "guest articles," as long as the subject is educational and interesting to their readers. Your article can inform readers on a topic related to your business or, if your work is unique, you may be permitted to author a feature on your company. At the least, most editors will allow a bio note about you and your company at the end of the article.

Robert Kullman of Kullman Industries, a commercial construction company in Avenel, N.J., wrote about a synagogue project they completed. That article made the front page of the *New York Times* real-estate section and led to a $10-million deal.

The company has written and placed more than a half-dozen articles in trade journals covering industries in which it was trying to build market share. Recent stories appearing in *American School and University,* for example, brought Kullman a private-school project worth $2 million.

234
IDEA

Publicity Seeding

Seek publicity and gain credibility in the marketplace by **seeding high-profile enthusiastic users who will endorse your product or service**.

Magellan Systems of San Dimas, Calif., had a low budget to prove the abilities of the lifesaving global positioning by satellite (GPS) navigational instruments it manufactures. Traditional advertising wouldn't give them credibility, and they couldn't afford to hire a public relations agency. So, Richard Sill, Magellan's vice-president of marketing, decided to "seed" their units to key hobbyists, professionals, and journalists—people who could grasp the technology quickly and might be willing to explain it to others.

For the cost of one magazine ad, they could hand out six units to such people. The recipients of the units included the editor of a boating magazine, a South African adventurer, the president of the New York Botanical Garden, and an individual making a record-breaking crossing of the Atlantic in a solar-powered vessel.

Magellan's calculated giveaways paid handsome dividends. The editor gave its GPS an enthusiastic review, and the other high-profile recipients helped garner free publicity for the instrument. In Magellan's first (but incomplete) fiscal year, sales were $1 million. Seven years later, they had reached $70 million.

235

IDEA

Heat Up the Press

Instead of bombarding every food writer in the world with press releases, East Coast Grill **targeted the journalists** who would be most likely to write about its new bottled hot sauce.

Boone Pendergrast, a former employee of the Cambridge, Mass., restaurant who was commissioned to publicize Inner Beauty Real Hot Sauce, had no formal background in sales, but that didn't stop him. His first stop was the Boston Public Library, where he searched a database of articles written on peppers in the last three years. The search, which cost nothing, took only an hour and yielded a list of about 85 food writers and editors around the country. For about $200, Pendergrast mailed each a bottle of Inner Beauty and a one-page press release that began "Inner Beauty Hot Sauce, hottest sauce in North America, unleashed on general public..."

Within six months, Inner Beauty Hot Sauce had garnered mention in half a dozen magazines, including *Metropolitan Home, Family Circle,* and *Condé Nast Traveler.* The coverage, Pendergrast believes, earned Inner Beauty more than just free exposure. "The difference between advertising and having your product mentioned in an article is credibility," he says. Pendergrast estimated that he spent $6,000 on direct marketing in three years since his first targeted mailing. And this year, wholesale sales of the sauce will approach $200,000. Inner Beauty Real Hot Sauce appears everywhere, from the Four Seasons Hotel in Chicago to George's sausage cart outside Fenway Park in Boston.

"The aristocracy have always been entrepreneurs. 'Aristocracy' is a Greek word that means the rule of the best— those who are better qualified. Aristocrats had to defend the village against intruders when the Mongols were invading. In that sense, entrepreneurship is really the same thing. Business is about ruling and having responsibilities."

HEINRICH VON LIECHTENSTEIN
executive director of the
European Foundation for Entrepreneurship

236
IDEA

Talk Show Cameo

Here's a no-cost way to get on the radio: **Call in to talk shows**. You may get a chance to tell thousands of people what you do, even if the topic of discussion is not related to your business.

Ben Levitan, author of *Too Easy Gourmet,* a cookbook, listens to drive-time local talk radio and often calls in. One day a radio show host was discussing how obnoxious people could be when using cellular phones. Levitan called in to defend himself and fellow mobile-phone users, telling the audience how his phone is the life of his business.

"When the host asked about my business," says Levitan, "I gave him my 10-second spiel: *'Too Easy Gourmet, The World's First Non-Fiction Cookbook,* recipes with five ingredients, 20 minutes or less, for one.' They were so interested they invited me to be on the show the next day. I sold 500 books."

237 IDEA

Good Citizen

Chris Zane's parents raised him with the expectation that he would give something back to the community, and he has. But the owner of Zane's Cycles, a $1.5-million bicycle dealer in Branford, Conn., also discovered that **being a good citizen is good business**.

When Connecticut passed a bike-helmet law in 1992, Zane persuaded Trek to help him offer kids' $40 helmets at cost ($20). "Indirectly, we profited because we did something for the community," says Zane. "We also got a lot of publicity, and that boosted sales." The cost of the helmet program: $0.

Zane also started the Zane Foundation, which awards five $1,000 college scholarships to Branford High School seniors. Since 1989, he has financed the scholarships with revenues generated by 50 candy machines scattered throughout the Branford area. All are labeled with Zane Foundation placards. After an initial investment of $2,500, Zane says, the program has paid for itself. "We're doing something our competitors and the category-killers aren't," adds Zane. "If people see that we're taking care of the community, they're more likely to come to us."

238
IDEA

Making Sponsorships Count

Sponsoring community events, charities, and nonprofit organizations can build goodwill for your business and enlarge your customer base. But your charitable time and money will be wasted unless you **make your sponsorship visible before, during, and after the event**.

Bennett Gibbs of Bennett's Cycle, in Minneapolis, makes sure his $200,000 retail store is noticed when he sponsors cycling events. At a recent Iron Man ride, a 100-mile event for 5,700 hard-core bike riders, Bennett's opened its door for registration prior to the event and offered participants six seminars on fitness and bicycle maintenance.

At the Iron Man, the company handed out bags filled with bike accessories and discount coupons for bike tune-ups and helmets. An offer was printed on the outside, giving shoppers 20% off anything they could fit in the bag. Within a week of last year's Iron Man, 30 participants had come into the store. After several weeks, Gibbs observed that 2,500 of the 5,300 participants had purchased goods at Bennett's Cycle.

"We support them and they support us," says Gibbs, whose business has become a 16,000-square-foot retail and repair shop with annual revenues of $3 million.

239

IDEA

Picture in the Newspaper

Some CEOs are too shy to play spokesperson. And then there's Pete Slosberg, founder of Pete's Brewing, in Palo Alto, Calif.

Slosberg's publicity pro, Kristin Seuell, came up with the idea to celebrate one million cases sold and got Slosberg to pose for a newspaper publicity shot in a bathtub, surrounded by his liquid assets. But rather than just send the photo and a press release scattershot to newspapers, she filed the photo with PhotoWire, a commercial service of Business Wire, which **sends photos digitally into the darkrooms of more than 370 newspapers** as well as ABC and CNN. The caption: "Specialty brewers make it from bathtub to big time."

The color photo was picked up by 35 papers, including the *San Francisco Chronicle, Arizona Republic,* and *Orlando Sentinel.* The filing cost: $725, which was "worth every cent," says Seuell.

Insuring the Jackpot

Imagine the publicity you would receive if you offered a $10,000 prize for an event. If you can't even imagine having $10,000 to give away, you might not have to. You can cover a grand prize that is awarded on risk by purchasing an insurance policy at a fraction of the cost.

When Instant Copy of Indiana Inc. was asked to help sponsor the Hoosier Celebrities Golf Tournament for $1,000, Jack Caffray said no. Instead, the president of the $11-million printing company **offered a $10,000 prize** to any golfer who hit a hole in one on the ninth hole—$5,000 would go to the golfer and $5,000 to the charity. Caffray then paid $750 for a premium from Lloyd's of London to insure himself against a potential $10,000 loss. That cost him $250 less than if he had been a regular sponsor.

The prize was announced repeatedly by the local newspapers, television stations, and radio stations, which treated the event and the prize as news. On the day of the tournament, a sign depicting a $10,000 check was erected behind the ninth hole, a target for television cameras during the event. The biggest winner of the day was Jack Caffray, who received a tremendous amount of free publicity despite the fact that no one won the prize.

241
IDEA

More Than a Free Sample

Journalists are accustomed to sampling products and services free from companies seeking their review. James Knowles, however, goes a step further to encourage the media to write articles about The Roger Smith Hotel in New York, which he took over in 1988.

Like most hotels, The Roger Smith offers a free room to travel writers when they're in town. But to really get their attention, Knowles hosts a "media slumber party," beginning with a wine reception and dinner, followed by unconventional entertainment. The night ends with journalists "sleeping over" in a penthouse.

Knowles also **hosts events for art industry journalists and enthusiasts**, positioning his hotel as a favorite spot for the art world. The Roger Smith Hotel is home to the "Aurora Series"—an annual creative gala of poetry readings, storytelling, plays, musical performances, and culinary events.

Knowles' activities have brought his hotel more than its share of press coverage and word-of-mouth advertising. As a result, revenues for The Roger Smith have continually increased, even at times when business has been dismal for other New York hotels.

242 IDEA

Publicity Builds Database

Tony Manzi, president and founder of Have Book, Will Travel, in Wilton, Conn., figured that if people took the trouble to write to him, they would read what he sends back and become potential mail-order customers. His theory proved correct, and Manzi has **built a database of ideal customers by getting them to write first**. Instead of advertising or mailing catalogs to purchased lists, Manzi gets his names by offering a free "Travel Packing List" of 100 items one might want to consider for a trip along with a trifold brochure, to anyone who sends a self-addressed stamped envelope. It costs him nothing to send the brochure and information about his "best books" service.

If a customer provides Have Book, Will Travel with a destination or activity, this innovative mail-order company prepares a list of best books from a database. Each list provides the title, price, and description of each book. This saves customers the time it might take to do research themselves. Also, they save money, since Manzi's prices are 10% off retail.

The two elements of his business, the unique service and the free list, attract publicity. Manzi writes his own press releases and distributes them without the help of publicists or media experts. His efforts led to articles printed in over 50 publications, resulting in more than 6,000 requests for his brochure. Subsequently, many of the recipients placed orders, and their names were used for future mailings.

Eight Ideas for Free Publicity

You can get your fifteen minutes of fame—along with new customers or clients—by describing to the media something you've done that's innovative, funny, or evokes human interest. Here are **eight ways to make yourself newsworthy**, according to Marcia Yudkin, Ph.D., Boston-based writing consultant and author of *Six Steps to Free Publicity*:

1. Concoct an interesting characterization of yourself. Rick Davis of Temple, N.H., created "The Institute of Totally Useless Skills."
2. Present your ordinary program or service to an unexpected clientele (prisoners, kids).
3. Piggyback on the news or current entertainment. For example, during the summer of 1993 when *Jurassic Park* was playing everywhere, anything about dinosaurs appeared timely.
4. Write to newspaper columnists, agreeing or disagreeing with them.
5. Conduct business in an unusual setting—hold your awards dinner at the zoo, or conduct a board meeting in the mailroom.
6. Break a record. *The Guinness Book of World Records* sells a million copies a year.
7. Do something anachronistic (make house calls; answer your own phone; bring back glass bottles).
8. Take the lead in complying with new legislation (such as the Americans with Disabilities Act).

All Aboard for Training

Westcon, a New York City distributor of computer-network hardware and purveyor of network technical training, bought itself four **uninterrupted hours of access to several dozen potential customers and trade-press journalists**. How? By renting a train his clients had to use anyway.

Bruce Hanson, vice president of Westcon, knew that journalists, customers, and prospects would use an Amtrak train to get from Manhattan to Boston for an industry trade show. So Westcon chartered and catered a coach car. In one part of the car, Westcon instructors finished the second half of a daylong training course that had started in New York City earlier in the morning. They called it Training on the Train and sent out invitations that looked like boarding passes.

The $4,000 promotional event was cheaper than throwing a dinner party. What's more, it had some practical purposes—not just training but transportation as well—and it was unique. "We were trying to establish that we were more innovative than the competition," says Hanson, who later put another Westcon training train on the tracks to Washington, D.C.

Spotlight on Charities

Here's a way to **increase sales, get favorable publicity**, and attract dedicated and like-minded employees. Leib Ostrow, CEO of Music for Little People in Redway, Calif., promoted nonprofit groups "that provide help to the planet" in his mail-order catalog of cassettes, videotapes, and musical instruments for children.

Customer feedback was 100-to-1 in favor, Ostrow said. And for at least three of the 12 nonprofit groups spotlighted over three years, the catalog was the single most important source of new members.

"These causes are struggling to get started, just like growing businesses. They've experienced funding cuts, and it's up to entrepreneurs to support them," said Ostrow.

246
IDEA

Send a Fax, Save the Earth

To woo prospects who may be reluctant to read press releases, **turn your PR text into a public service announcement**—and watch the responses roll in.

Marketing consultant Wendy Zaritsky developed a public relations strategy of sending broadcast faxes to media throughout the southwest, to generate low-cost exposure for Barbara Rishel's new book, *Earth-Friendly Living*. The fax was more of a public service announcement than a press release—it offered a free copy of a brochure listing hundreds of hotline phone numbers for the environmentally responsible citizen.

In addition to providing a valuable public service, Zaritsky gained the names of hot prospects for the book: people who sent in a self-addressed stamped envelope to receive the brochure. From just one fax broadcast session, her offer was mentioned in more than 30 publications. Some 200 people requested a free brochure, of whom 13% responded to the book offer that came with it.

247
IDEA

R$_X$ for Disaster

Don't wait until you're in crisis to whip up a public-relations strategy. **Have a crisis publicity plan ready in advance**.

Elliot Sainer, CEO of Aspen Health Services, a wilderness therapy program for troubled teens in Huntington Beach, Calif., already had a publicity plan at work when a teenager died while attending a competitor's program. Still, Aspen had to beef up efforts to battle the onslaught of bad press.

As kids withdrew from Aspen's program and new-business calls dropped by 20%, Sainer added an employee to his in-house public relations team. Already busy touting Aspen's safety record, the team sped up the distribution of information on graduates' progress and turned the annual newsletter into a quarterly.

Next, Sainer agreed to a story request from *U.S. News & World Report.* "We were seeing our industry getting slammed," he said. He allowed the reporter to join one group at the end of its program, when the participating teens are happiest. Sainer was pleased with the article and mailed copies to more than 200 referral sources. A year later, Aspen was back on track, with about $6 million in revenues and incoming calls back to normal. Sainer credited the company's survival to its PR strategy.

Press for Effective E-Mail

E-mail is a terrific way to distribute press releases with immediacy. But before you hit the "send" key, make sure your message is well-written and easy to read—so that recipients don't respond with their "delete" key before even attempting to read it.

Eric Ward, principal of the Ward Group—a firm that specializes in news sharing for Web launches and Web-based events—offers **key tips to make your e-mail press release as effective and "reader-friendly"** as possible.

- Never send untargeted mass mailings of any type. Know your audience, and respect it.
- Compose your releases using the ASCII character-set, or, if you don't know how, compose in standard Courier typeface, in 10-point font size. Then, type no more than 65 characters per line, hitting the "return" key to begin each and every new line.
- Add your e-mail address.
- Include the URL in a prominent location, also on its own line. Don't try to make the URL stand out with all capital letters, and don't leave off the http:// prefix.
- Always indicate where your recipients can find the press release online if it exists at your company Web site. For a sample Web page press release, visit http://www.urlwire.com/docs/samplepr.html.
- Use a descriptive subject line in your e-mail. Don't type the words "PRESS RELEASE" in your subject line with no other description. Instead, type headlines such as "ACME Launches RoadRunner Server v2.0, Free Download Available."

XIV

"You sell a company twice.
First of all, you sell
them the product, then you
sell them the service."

RICHARD BROCK
founder, chairman, and CEO of
Brock Control Systems

Learn to Read Customers

Do you **emphasize the aspect of your product or service that most appeals to an individual client**? Millard Choate, CEO of Choate Construction in Marietta, Ga., learned the hard way how important that is.

While his company was growing from $17 million to $136 million in five years, the speed with which he completed jobs was a strong selling point. Yet, one potential customer was not impressed. "We showed this company slides of buildings we'd done in a short period of time," said Choate. He was shocked when his proposal was rejected. "They said our company was more powerful than what they wanted. They wanted to go at a sleepier pace." If he had known that earlier, he could have marketed another aspect of the company's expertise in building. The lesson he took out of it was, read your clients as much as you can.

250
IDEA

New Customers at Cost

Here's one way to start relationships with new customers: **Sell them your products at cost**. Sound crazy? Not to Peachpit Press, a small publisher in Berkeley, Calif., that announced it was selling, at cost, 77,000 copies of its then-latest book, *Zap! How Your Computer Can Hurt You and What You Can Do About It*. The book lists for $12.95, but corporations that ordered it within four months of publication would pay just 90 cents a copy for a minimum order of 30.

In planning its promotion, Peachpit called several corporations. A safety manager liked the preview enough to order 300 copies for her own company; she also alerted her industry group. That led to an order for 3,000 copies. More orders came in as the offer went public in newspapers and trade journals. Within four weeks, Peachpit had heard from more than 30 corporations. IBM, Wells Fargo, Gillette, and *USA Today* placed orders. They were all new customers Peachpit would never have reached through conventional retail channels.

Sales manager Keasley Jones called the *Zap!* promotion more beneficial and more measurable than any other marketing he's tried, including image advertising. "We know the benefits: exposure to a new niche and new customers."

Warranties Increase, Sales Increase

Warranties and guarantees reassure prospective buyers and build trust with your customers. Some companies have found that **when you increase the length of your warranty, you can also increase sales and referrals**.

Paul Eldrenkamp, president and founder of a home remodeling business in Newton, Mass., stumbled upon this truth when his company needed a boost. He sent a letter to 40 past clients asking to take a look at his work because his company, Byggmeister Inc., was thinking of instituting a five-year warranty. Over the next few weeks he visited former clients in their homes.

He thought he might be on to something when he saw customer referrals go up 30% in the first nine months. Even better, since they were referrals from his clients, rather than from architects soliciting multiple bids, he was more likely to get the job as the only contractor in the picture.

The results were so impressive that now, when Byggmeister completes a job, Eldrenkamp promises the client that if anything goes wrong, he'll take care of it. If a year goes by and Eldrenkamp hasn't heard anything, he checks in anyway. The payoff, in repeat business and rave referrals, is huge. Sales went up 25% in a year, and in three years, revenue doubled.

Successfully Rejecting Business

It's hard to tell a prospective client, "I'm not right for this job." But Phyllis Apelbaum, president of Arrow Messenger Service in Chicago, found that when you **turn business down for the right reason** and in the right way, very often it will come back to you.

Twenty-three years ago, when Arrow was starting out, a national package delivery company offered Apelbaum a $500,000 contract to be its Chicago-based pickup point. "The truth was," says Apelbaum, "we were too small. I went back and said, 'I appreciate the opportunity. We're not the right vendor to do this.' It was very painful to turn away the largest piece of work that had come my way."

A few years after the fateful $500,000 question, Apelbaum got to bid on another large contract. Neiman Marcus was coming to Chicago and needed a courier company. Apelbaum's anecdote about turning down a similar contract until she was ready was a great selling point. She convinced the department store that she understood what it took to service a big account, and even offered the other company as a reference.

253
IDEA

Take 'Em Out to the Ballgame

How do you fill a room with prospects? **Try hosting an event that matches your clients' interests.**

Geoff Allen, CEO, and Jeff Gordon, chairman of Source Digital, a value-added reseller and integrator of video-editing systems in Vienna, Va., had no trouble gathering 128 corporate prospects last September. The occasion: an Orioles vs. Red Sox match at Camden Yards.

The partners rented out an old warehouse next to right field. While the batters warmed up outside, the corporate crowd munched on barbecued chicken inside. Allen and Gordon got the prospects' attention by showing, on two large screens, how a baseball coach could use the latest video-editing technology in training. The group asked questions and filled out a survey rating the sales presentation and the technology.

Afterward, everyone headed to the stands. The Orioles prevailed—and so did Source Digital. Two months after hosting the $15,000 event (paid for in part by vendor co-op marketing funds), the $10-million company closed six deals worth $420,000. Says Allen, "It was a good day for the clients, for us, and for the Orioles."

Prospects, Meet Our Customers

Consumers who are contemplating a complex contract or big-ticket purchase may need some reassurance before they buy. You can give it to them by having satisfied customers sing your praises.

In addition to a fine-tuned sales pitch and a tour of his facilities, Ned Lamont, CEO of TeleVideo in Greenwich, Conn., **brought prospects face-to-face with existing customers**. He believed such testimonials were much stronger when given in person.

Lamont used this tactic to help increase his business from three to eleven contracts five years later. During an installation of his cable-television system at Kent State, for example, Campus TeleVideo invited representatives from five Ohio-area schools to drop in; they did and had lots of questions. Not long after that, Lamont was invited to bid on three Ohio college contracts—and won.

Technicians Can Sell

Are you overlooking hidden, knowledgeable sales talent at your warehouse or R&D labs? **Technical employees can double as sales people with the right training**. They can accurately describe the product, answer customers' questions knowledgeably, and take what they learn from customers back to the design and production labs. That's why ERM Program Management in Exton, Pa., relies on engineers to sell their products and services.

Before sending scientists and engineers into the trenches, CEO Jack Newell hired a marketing manager to direct the efforts of the technical staff. He also paid for the group to take communications classes to learn the basics of selling.

Twenty senior scientists and engineers now compete for bonuses worth as much as 50% of their base salary. The bonuses are tied to new-business targets, billable hours, and other goals, such as presenting a certain number of technical papers. The scientists are paid out twice a year, provided the company meets its overall profitability goal. The company has done so for the last three years.

256
IDEA

Selling Through Key Influencers

When you've got a great but unfamiliar product or service that's difficult to advertise, try an engineered "word-of-mouth" marketing campaign. Begin by **offering samples to people who influence your target market**.

That's how Michael Stusser, owner of Osmosis in Freestone, Calif., marketed the first enzyme bath in America. He knew if people tried it, word would spread. For 30 years the Japanese have enjoyed the health and stress-relieving benefits of an enzyme bath, yet this product was unknown in the United States.

Stusser decided to offer a free enzyme bath to local massage therapists, acupuncturists, and other alternative health practitioners, who were in a position to recommend what's best for their clients' bodies and health, and whose target market was the same as his. The results were terrific. Within two months, 25 to 30 people had been referred by only two of the acupuncturists who had tried the bath. Eleven years later, his 20-employee business is thriving, and Michael hosts a reception for his influencers each year to maintain the goodwill.

Picture This

If you can help apprehensive clients "picture" what they are about to buy, you may find yourself with a signed contract.

Portugal-based Web designer Patrick M. van der Valk **mocks up a sample Web page** with his prospect's name and logo and presents it to them on his laptop during the sales pitch. He brings up their competitors' sites in his Web browser, then shows them how theirs could look if he designed it. Since van der Valk started his business in 1995, he has achieved an 85% acceptance rate for his proposals.

J. Ratto, a landscaping contractor in Medford, N.Y., had a hard time convincing clients to hire him—until he used Bissett Nursery's computer-imaging service. Instead of showing prospective clients plants in a book, or hand-drawing blueprints, Ratto now takes a picture of their houses and plots Bissett's plants in the picture. "Before this technology existed, clients had a hard time envisioning everything and were still hesitant," recalls Ratto. In two years since the new system was adopted, Ratto has more than doubled his residential sales, and $25-million wholesaler Bissett Nursery has generated $13 million in additional sales.

"At Wabash, everybody sinks
or swims together—everybody,
even our salespeople. They aren't
on commission. They participate
in the same compensation system
as everybody else."

JERRY EHRLICH
CEO of Wabash National

258
IDEA

Charity Begins at Work

For a discerning marketer, a charitable contribution can also serve as a sales opportunity. American Ophthalmic in Winter Park, Fla., a chain of ophthalmic clinics and surgery centers, **gave free eye screenings and handed out literature to Meals on Wheels** senior centers. Employees also participated in health fairs, fundraisers, and food drives run by the nonprofits.

During visits to Meals on Wheels centers, American Ophthalmic's certified technicians checked vision, and its doctors made presentations about the aging eye. Screenings were free, but the company made money when people signed up for full exams or required surgery. CEO Thomas Whatley estimated that his various community-outreach programs (which also included elementary school visits) brought in about 25% of his sales.

Resourceful Prospecting

You're an expert in your industry, so why not package that expertise for customers? Serving as a resource does take time, but it's a great prospecting tool.

Flexible Personnel, a $60-million staffing company headquartered in Fort Wayne, Ind., **transformed its employment law know-how into a labor-law seminar**. "We thought this would be worth a lot more to our customers than the coffee mugs and key chains our industry typically hands out," says agency president Doug Curtis.

His clients agree. Nearly 800 customers and prospects come to his seminars (four free all-day sessions) armed with questions about complex labor laws. A paid consultant and Flexible's lawyer lead the discussion. After one seminar, the agency received 45 new job orders totaling roughly $500,000 and picked up a customer Flexible had pursued for three years.

260 IDEA

Repeat Business Bonus

I'd like to invite every customer over for dinner—that's how you feel when you own a company. But how do you get employees to treat the customer like that?" wondered Elliot Goodwin, president of Larry's Shoes, a chain of men's shoe stores with headquarters in Fort Worth, Texas. So that employees would feel they had a vested interest in their clients, and help build repeat business, he created incentives for his sales force—the people who would keep customers coming back.

First, Goodwin **added 3% to the salespeople's commissions for customers who returned within a year**. He also supplied his full-time sales force with business cards, thank-you notes, birthday cards, and the like, to encourage ongoing connections.

Marketing director Terry Hillgartner concludes, "The single most important factor in maintaining existing customers is our follow-up program. Thank-you cards to every customer are a must, along with notifying customers of sales and new products when they arrive."

261 IDEA

Mingle While You Work

Networking at business and social events is one of the most effective ways to achieve word-of-mouth advertising, referrals, and clients. Susan RoAne, author of *How to Work a Room* (Warner Books, 9th ed., 1989), offers some **guidelines for successful mingling**:

- Come prepared with business cards and a pen. Keep track of new connections by writing on the back of their business cards.
- Describe your business in one or two sentences, and make it memorable by giving a benefit.
- Develop several different ways to start conversations, such as commenting on the event or asking people to tell you something about themselves.
- Try to spend no more than 10 minutes with each person you meet.
- Listen more than you talk.
- Listen for a need, and be a good lead or referral whenever possible.
- Be positive, friendly, enthusiastic, and have fun!
- Follow up with the people you meet, and the contacts they give you, in a timely manner.

Turn Reps into Entrepreneurs

John Nugent and Tony Baudanza, founders of Pivot Point Inc., in Woburn, Mass., knew that to make their imprint on the software industry, they'd need a lot of "feet on the street." Their biggest phobia: the cost of sales. Their solution: **get superstar salespeople to start their own company** to represent Spectrum software as its sole line.

After Spectrum had reached 200 customers, and sales were climbing toward $3.5 million, the partners persuaded six top-rated salespeople from other software companies (including several of their selling partners) to fork over their own money to cover rent, demo gear, and salaries. Spectrum put down nothing, but agreed to help out in a cash crunch. The reps won an exclusive territory, fat commissions (50% of gross sales), and control. "We provided good sales forecasts that showed how they could have a $6-million business in a few years," adds Nugent.

Nugent and Baudanza went on to inspire the creation of seven more rep firms around the country, taking a minority interest in several. Each time, reps kicked in $10,000 to $40,000 apiece. Spectrum's sales have increased more than tenfold since the company launched its first rep group. Thanks to that channel, Spectrum's selling costs are only 25% of sales, compared with competitors' 50% to 60%.

Borrowing Your Salesperson

Switching from commodity selling to value-added selling requires a whole new understanding of customer expectations. For G&F Industries, a small manufacturer of molded-plastic parts in Sturbridge, Mass., the new approach meant no selling at all—at least, in the traditional sense.

G&F's largest account—Bose, a $700-million acoustic-speaker maker in nearby Framingham—asked if G&F would consider **assigning a full-time employee to work at their plant**, eliminating the need for a salesperson to call and helping Bose shave the cost of buyers and planners.

It was a risky move for little G&F, which at the time barely cleared $3 million in sales. President John Argitis had some sleepless nights before agreeing to give it a try. "This has changed our whole way of doing business, but I never thought it would work this well," he now says. "Instead of spending time trying to get new accounts, we concentrate solely on servicing and pricing. You don't really sell, you look for opportunities."

In the ten years since adopting the new approach, sales have been close to $15 million and G&F has grown 25% to 40% a year, on average, despite a depressed plastics industry at times.

264
IDEA

Fly In Your Customers

To impress prospects on its own turf, Rite-Hite, a manufacturer of loading-dock equipment in Milwaukee, pays for a fly-in program to **educate its customers' quality and safety teams**, as well as product users. When guests tour the factory they kick the tires of 100 pieces of equipment, including 40 competitors' models.

The tours help visitors identify their needs and explore possible solutions. About 90% of fly-in prospects eventually buy from Rite-Hite, says program director Robert Staehler. Within a year, 353 companies purchased $12 million worth of equipment. Costs, including follow-up after the tour, totaled $250,000. And Rite-Hite's value soared from $40 million to $250 million in nine years.

If you consider this prospecting strategy, Staehler suggests the following:

- Start small. Invite only those who will influence the buying decision. Stock a few key competitors' products, and expand as you grow.
- Share the cost. Back in 1988, Rite-Hite reps invited just 37 companies and paid the entire travel bill; now they pay half.
- Set benchmarks. "A minimum 50% closing ratio is good if you keep costs in line," says Staehler. "If you can't meet that, stay with more traditional marketing."
- Skip the frills. "This doesn't have to be lavish," he says. "They come because they're scared of making the wrong decision."

265
IDEA

Reach Out and Sell Someone

With the cost of an in-person industrial sales visit averaging $160 to $180, more and more **companies are using the telephone as a less costly sales tool**. That's why the salespeople at Amekor Industries rarely travel outside the Conshohocken, Pa., headquarters. In one month, this distributor of wigs and hair goods rang up over $500,000 worth of sales on a $5,000 phone bill. Stephen Perchick, chairman of the company, puts the cost of an average phone sales call at five dollars.

One of Amekor's secrets to selling a product unseen is by starting new customers off with a small order of samples. Salespeople pitch a select number of products, instead of trying to sell the whole product line on the first call. They offer to send product samples, along with brochures and other detailed material.

"Once you understand your customer's market, you can try selling them a larger cross-section of products," says Perchick. Perchick claims to have a 90% reorder rate with new accounts that have purchased initial samples.

266
IDEA

Electronic Dragnet

With a mere $150 worth of desktop computer software, you can reach all the customers in a target area and plot their location on a map—in minutes!

John Paul Mitchell Systems **finds and maps its target customers using Select Street Atlas and Select Phone software** from Pro CD of Danvers, Mass. Veny Musum, the hair products company's senior vice president, plugs the Standard Industry Classification (SIC) code for hair salons into Select Phone, limits the search by ZIP code or county, and feeds the addresses into Street Atlas to plot a map for his salespeople. The process takes about five minutes.

Once Musum began using the software, he was dismayed to find his company had penetrated only a fourth of the market. Salespeople reported they had 300 to 400 accounts in Queens, one of New York City's five boroughs. When Musum searched Select Phone, he located over 2,000 salons in the area. The sales force received a plotted map of the new leads. With this information, Musum believes his company will quadruple its sales.

Get the Team in the Field

When Ann Machado **uses team selling to win the big accounts**, she really means team. The CEO of Creative Staffing Inc., a $15-million staffing firm in Miami, fields a lineup for clients that often includes herself, her chief financial officer, her sales director, the sales rep, the operations manager, and the person who will service the account.

Says Machado: "When you explain what each person does, it gives you more credibility." Customers agree that it's great to sit across the table from all the players because they know who's going to carry out the service.

Machado, who spends 10% of her time on team presentations, says the tactic lowers selling costs. Previously, it took as long as six months to close a major deal; now it takes as little as five weeks because the team gathers critical information more quickly. While the CFO tackles issues such as workers' comp, the sales director can assess the fit between the two companies.

There are a few drawbacks to team pitching: there is limited time available to establish a rapport, and in an hour meeting, you can overwhelm the prospect. However, Machado says her team usually leaves with a small order that day. Team selling—proven successful by big companies like Xerox—has netted Creative Staffing new contracts worth over $250,000 each. Also, two million-dollar accounts, under attack by a competitor, were saved by Machado's team.

268

IDEA

Hiring the Influential

Jill Griffin, author of *Customer Loyalty: How to Earn It, How to Keep It* (Lexington Books, 1995), and president of the Marketing Resource Center in Austin, Texas, suggests turning people of influence into full-time advocates. The strategy: **Hire employees who know the people who will purchase from you**.

When Jay Stein started his first boutique in Greensville, Miss., he hired well-to-do women who had lived in the area for years to be his influential associates. When Stein decided to liquidate designer clothing one year, several affluent local women volunteered to help. They had firsthand knowledge of this better merchandise, because they had worn it for years. When Stein opened his next store in Memphis, he and his wife recruited socialite women to operate it.

"Boutique Ladies," as they are now called, have become status symbols and hold coveted positions in Stein Marts throughout the country. Their activities are focused on spreading the word about the merchandise. For example, when a shipment of designer silk separates arrived in the Jacksonville location, boutique lady Joy Abney called her fellow board members at the Wolfson Children's Hospital. Abney's friends spent $2,000 in her store that day.

"On busy days in our telemarketing centers, I bring in buffet lunches, so people don't have to get up from their stations to go to lunch. But I haven't yet gotten them to accept the catheter idea I proposed."

JIM McCANN
CEO of 800-FLOWERS

269
IDEA

Two-Tier Telemarketing

With $1.5 million in sales, CWC Software in Braintree, Mass., can't afford to put a salesperson on the road. So, the eight-year-old company—which sells a subscription-fulfillment program called QuickFill—makes strategic use of telemarketing, **dividing its phone sales force into two prospectors and one "closer."**

The prospectors are less expensive part-timers who don't need detailed product knowledge or finely honed selling skills. They make the initial contact with people who respond to CWC ads. "They make sure that prospects received the demo disk they asked for," says vice-president Bill Bean, "and encourage them to open it and try it." The prospectors also answer the most commonly asked questions.

When prospects start to look like buyers, their names go onto the "hot" list. The seasoned closer—an experienced salesperson with extensive product knowledge—then takes that list, answers very specific questions, and lobbies everyone who must approve the purchase at the prospect's company.

Using this two-tiered approach, CWC has steadily increased its leads and sales. Some telemarketers, however, believe you should have two closers for every prospector—a ratio that Bean will consider once CWC's revenues grow a bit larger. For now he's content to see the company both in the black and meeting sales projections.

Silver Spurs

Accelerated commission schemes and fancy bonus plans have their place, but there are other, less formal ways to motivate your sales force. Smart CEOs know that **well-timed surprises or individually tailored perks can do a lot to inspire salespeople** between January and December. Here are a couple of creative reward programs:

RazorSoft International, Oklahoma City, a developer and distributor of video games, ranked its nine salespeople monthly on the basis of gross profit. Number one received a $500 bonus (on top of commission) and the best office in the department. Even number eight got $50. CEO Kyle Shelley used to base the bonus on gross sales, but since he switched to profits, gross profits as a percentage of sales grew by 16%.

Professional Salon Concepts in Joliet, Ill., a supplier of hair-care products and educational training for salon owners, encouraged its 15 salespeople by offering $200 Nordstrom gift certificates to the two sellers "who touched the biggest number of current and prospective clients" in a month. Performance was measured by customer classes taught, cold calls, appointments, and visits. The average number of visits per month increased from 115 before the contest to 148 a year later. And, an added benefit, the sales logs gave executives a chance to analyze everyone's time management.

Shoe-In Stunt

No matter how many sales calls you make, sometimes **it may take something bold like a humorous stunt to get through to your prospect**. After two years and dozens of unreturned calls to the executive director of a large trade association, Mike MacNair, president of $10-million MacNair Travel Management in Alexandria, Va., did something different to obtain an appointment.

MacNair stopped by his local Goodwill store and picked up a pair of black wingtip shoes. He shined one of the shoes to perfection, gift-wrapped it, and had the package delivered to the prospect. When the executive director opened the box, he found a handwritten note that read (in part): "I'm trying to get my foot in the door..."

The unique "gift" put a smile on the prospect's face. He returned MacNair's next call and agreed to their first meeting. His trade association now spends $80,000 a year through MacNair's travel agency.

272

IDEA

Cash In on Cold Calling

When it comes to cold calls, perhaps the hardest step is that first one through the door. Chuck Piola, top seller at NCO Financial Systems, a $80-million collection agency in Blue Bell, Pa., **motivates himself to make cold calls by attaching a dollar value to every call**. He got the idea from a book published in 1947, *How I Raised Myself from Failure to Success in Selling*.

In Piola's favorite passage, author Frank Bettger tells how he simply divided his yearly earnings by the number of calls he made, regardless of whether he saw the prospect or not, let alone closed a sale.

Doing the math like that has helped Piola walk through many a door, especially in his early days in the field. Whether you attempt it on a weekly, monthly, quarterly, or yearly basis, he says, "keeping track helps you realize you're getting better." In a career spanning more than 20,000 cold calls, Piola figures that every time he makes an entrance now, he has gotten the sales per call as high as $150.

Focus, Zoom, and Click

Cleo Belle Robertson, owner of CBR Associates in Durham, N.C., had amassed an impressive prospect list for the database-software program her company had developed for hospital administration. But her sales efforts went nowhere. Close to bankruptcy, she gambled on consultant David Beyer's **advice to focus and organize her sales efforts**.

Here's what Beyer taught Robertson:

- ◦ Eliminate bargain hunters by raising the price. Robertson upped the price of her software—from $6,000 to $9,000—to distinguish it as the best of its kind.
- ◦ Shrink the territory. Robertson had spread her resources thin by trying to sell nationwide. Instead, Beyer had her zero in on the 120 hospitals in North Carolina. The selling expenses amounted to the price of gas for a day's drive.
- ◦ Get the mail out. Five letters every other day to key people at each prospective hospital was Robertson's quota.
- ◦ Work the phones systematically. Beyer started Robertson on a regimen of six phone calls an hour, eventually increasing it to 100 calls a day. "I hated the phone," says Robertson, "but David drummed into me that it usually takes 10 calls to make a sale."

Focusing paid off. Within 30 days Robertson closed three sales. Eventually, 95% of the prospects she contacted bought the software program, PRIVplus. Her sales exceeded $335,000 during the first six months of that year—more than double the figure for the previous year.

Everyone Can Sell

Boosting sales is everybody's job at Telecom Library, headquartered in New York City. During a slow season, chairman Gerry Friesen shocked the 100-employee high-tech magazine publishing company by announcing that layoffs were inevitable unless **everyone pitched in with ideas for gaining more sales**.

Not only did the threat of layoffs get people's attention, but "the opportunity for them to work directly with me and show their stuff," says Friesen. He listened and asked questions. Then he told employees to flesh out their ideas or explained why they weren't feasible. For promising suggestions, he would always ask, "Do you have time to do this?" If employees said yes, they got the go-ahead.

The company pulled a "hat trick:"

- Editorial employees repackaged a dated but popular book to rejuvenate its sales.
- Sales staffers exchanged their 50 most-difficult-to-close accounts among themselves.
- The company got more mileage out of its editorial mailing list by using it to pull together a conference.

Six months later, though ad sales were still off, there were no layoffs, revenues went up, and the company became profitable.

275
IDEA

New Business Incentives

Distant goals and deferred rewards can result in disillusioned employees. That's why at Seattle-based Pacific Supply Co., workers take their bonuses one day at a time.

Every day that the apartment-supply company books $5,500 in sales, all 12 employees receive an extra half hour's pay. If daily sales hit $15,000, everyone racks up another six hours' wages. Using the previous year's sales as a benchmark, Pacific pays calculated bonuses once a month. The bonuses accrue daily and, in a typical month, amount to an extra 20 hours' salary for each employee.

Since Pacific **scrapped a monthly incentive program for a daily one**, sales have increased by more than half; turnover has plummeted to only one resignation in three years; and daily sales targets are hit four out of five days a week. Company president Michael Go says that because all employees share in the spoils, "instead of fostering individualism, we get a very high level of teamwork."

276
IDEA

Telephone Tag

When you get someone's voice mail and decide to leave a message, what can you do to ensure that your call will be returned? Lots, according to Jefferey Gitomer, author of *The Sales Bible* and president of Business Marketing Services in Charlotte, N.C.:

- Don't give your sales pitch on voice mail. Your objective is simply to make in-person or live telephone contact.
- Leave your number and first name only (in a very businesslike manner). Calls are returned in inverse proportion to the amount of information left by the caller.
- Be funny. Clean wit will get a response.
- Offer fun. For example, you could leave a message like this: "I have two extra tickets to the Knights game and I thought you might be interested. Please call me if you can't go so I can give the tickets to someone else."
- If you've had a positive first meeting, remind the prospect where you met.
- Dangle the carrot. **Leave just enough information to entice**. A similar tactic is to leave a half message and hang up. Cut your message short with something like, "Your name came up in a conversation with Hugh..." so the prospect will call back to find out the rest.
- Ask a provocative or thought-provoking question.

277
IDEA

Sales Force: Retired but Not Shy

When looking for midsize-company owners in need of his investment banking services, Steven Haupt believed in hanging out poolside. He created his own tailor-made **sales force of retired execs** who, while golfing or lounging at the club, agreed to listen for hot prospects.

"Small companies can't be reached through traditional sales tactics," insisted the CEO of S. J. Haupt & Co. "Often these CEOs don't know what an investment banker is." And while CEOs of public companies have to share numbers with the public, a lot of private-company owners tell more to their friends at the beach club than they do to their own management. Haupt's referral agents received 20% of all fees from any prospect-turned-client for their services. It was a profitable way for everyone to make a hole in one.

278
IDEA

Take the Limo to Lunch

Having trouble contacting customers at the CEO level? Bill Czapar, CEO of Anaheim Custom Extruders, waved goodbye to that problem with his "California Limo Lunch." Once a fellow CEO experienced the thrill of being whisked away to a restaurant in a chauffeured limo, future invitations were rarely refused. The lunches provided Czapar **regular opportunities to conduct business conversations without interruption**.

"I'm trying to pave the way so that if there is a problem with our product, we don't get thrown out for an occasional mistake," explained Czapar. He extended the lunch invitations about four times a year to the 20 customers most responsible for his annual sales of custom extruded plastics.

279
IDEA

Call-Back Guarantee

Are you losing customers because your salespeople don't return phone calls or respond too slowly to voice-mail messages? Tim Sharpe, vice president of sales for Absolute Graphics—an advertising specialty company in Stafford, Va.—has his salespeople guarantee that **customer calls will be returned in less than an hour**. If not, the customer receives a $25 gift certificate to a local restaurant, which is deducted from the salesperson's commission. Fortunately, Absolute Graphics' voice-mail system pages the salesperson as soon as there's a new message.

Most calls are returned within five minutes, claims Sharpe. And customers are quite impressed with such responsive service. Sharpe believes this policy prevents his customers from shopping around and keeps them coming back. And Absolute Graphics has had a polished track record: just one gift certificate was given out in two years since the guarantee was announced.

280

IDEA

Show Me Activity, I'll Show You Results

Despite a recession in the environmental cleanup industry, Cyn Environmental Services has consistently gained market share, increased profits, and expanded its operation. What's the secret? **Have a sales program that emphasizes activity over results**. "Lots of CEOs say to their salespeople, 'Show me results,' but this is counterproductive," says Bob Connelly, president of the Stoughton, Mass., hazardous-waste management business.

Connelly's sales strategy includes a step-by-step process to target, contact, and close ideal accounts. Salespeople are evaluated not on which accounts they close but, rather, on the progress they make toward building and developing relationships with potential clients. According to Connelly, when his salespeople follow the required steps, they almost always get in the door, and Cyn Environmental scores a new customer.

This activity-based sales motivation has helped grow the $20-million company 15% annually since 1991.

281
IDEA

I Read It in the News

Your best leads could be just 25 cents away—if that's how much your local newspaper costs. The *Washington Business Journal* is where Virginia Schaaf finds her leads to sell the graphic-design services of D.C.-based Don Schaaf and Friends.

Like most local newspapers, the *Business Journal* publishes announcements about new employees hired by local companies. Schaaf checks the newspaper each week for people newly hired in a marketing position. She then gets the address from the telephone book, sends an introductory letter with a company brochure, and follows up with a phone call a week later. Since they are new to their positions and want to make changes to marketing collateral, more than half of the recipients agree to an appointment.

Virginia's prospecting methods keep Don Schaaf's nine designers busy—over 25% of its business comes from **customers found in the newspaper**. How does she close so many sales? "I have a secret weapon," Ms. Schaaf says. "I happen to be Don's mom. People love that."

Growing with Customers

To grow your business, why not **focus on customers who are also growing** and will need more of your services? David Levy, principal and cofounder of Property Tax Specialists, bolstered the sales of his Silver Spring, Md., company by casting where more fish were swimming.

Until recently, most of PTS's customers were local property owners who were appealing tax assessments for the one or two properties they owned or managed. By 1994, Levy and partner Bill Quinn noticed that Real Estate Investment Trusts (REITs) were purchasing many of their clients' properties. PTS refocused its sales efforts on the REITs, which required more tax services as they bought and developed more properties.

After some hard work landing REITs as clients, PTS's proactive approach paid off. In two years, its sales have more than doubled, and REITs represent at least 25% of its revenue. PTS's portfolio of properties grew substantially without any incremental marketing time or costs.

283
IDEA

Brushing Up the Dentists

A strategy of convenience is how to get satisfied clients to refer business to you. Linda L. Miles, owner of a dental management and consulting company in Virginia Beach, Va., **focuses on making it easy and profitable for prospects to engage her services**.

Author of four books, Miles speaks at about 100 dental and health care conferences every year. Afterwards, she suggests to the meeting planner that he or she might be interested in earning her annual "Doctor of Distinction Award," which goes to the client who refers the most speaking or consulting business to her.

Miles hands her clients three prestamped postcards with information about her company and room for them to write a note to their dental-school colleagues or associate meeting planners. Each year, Miles gives out approximately 200 cards. She's convinced that the postcard strategy is one of the key factors that helped double her business, and she never has to work to get speaking engagements. "I am always scheduled a year in advance and I need to do little advertising to get new business," proclaims Miles.

A Healthy Source of Clients

Looking for new clients? Search no further than your local gym. It worked for Brooks E. Dabbs when he started Proactive Strategies, a marketing plan and analysis consultancy located near his gym in a key business area of Atlanta.

Many upper-level executives from companies in the area play basketball during weekday lunches and tennis on weekends at the club. Dabbs joins them on court and initiates conversations with all opponents and teammates during the workout, simply by asking, "What do you do?" From there, the discussion often leads, with direction from Dabbs, to marketing ideas and concepts.

The laid-back health club environment allows Dabbs to have an easy conversation about what his firm can provide and discuss his potential client's needs without the pressure of a sales call. His first tennis client is still providing business, and he is now in discussions with another potential client from another tennis match.

IDEA

Communication, Communication, Communication

Advanced Hardware Architectures, a semiconductor manufacturer in Pullman, Wash., needed to get the attention of independent sales representatives. To stand out in competition with their bigger, existing clients, president and CEO John Overby knew he would have to **get the company name and products in front of the representatives as frequently as possible**.

Each week, Overby's company faxes, mails, or e-mails a single-page newsletter to 75 representatives around the world. The publication introduces new products, recounts success stories, and offers selling tips for AHA products.

The repeat communication produces results. At sales meetings, the representatives comment that AHA is the only manufacturer to communicate so often, and they thank Overby for it. Eight years into the business, the company is approaching $20 million in sales.

286
IDEA

Specialize, the Referrals Will Follow

I n the day I sell. At night I work. The cycle never ends!" That was the complaint of Paul G. Lewis, CEO of a computer-network design and installation and support firm in Warren, N.J. Lewis was struggling to increase his sales because if he was working, he didn't have time to sell, and vice versa. He also couldn't afford to hire a salesperson. So, he decided to target customers who spoke to his potential client base every day and could recommend his company—thus becoming his **unpaid sales force**.

Lewis started spending his selling time with law and accounting firms. If he did a good job for them, he figured, they would mention his company to their clients and colleagues. He shone in his service for these clients, handed them a stack of his cards when he left, and asked them to recommend his company, MC^2, if they thought he had done a good job.

It didn't take long to see the results. Within two weeks of his first law firm job, a client was referred to him. That year sales grew a whopping 700% from the previous year, and his sales expense was zero. Eight years later, Lewis's revenues have reached $10 million.

Automation Without Tears

When moving your sales force from paper to PC, a little planning prevents disaster, according to George Colombo, author of *Sales Force Automation*. **Companies that became successfully automated followed this advice**:

- ➤ Involve salespeople early and give them time to adjust. They're more likely to use the system if they've helped design it. Companies that let information-system folks dictate the terms are often forced to start over.
- ➤ Use prototypes and trial runs. Salespeople won't know what they want right off the bat. So, consider giving them an inexpensive contact-management package for a trial period. From that will flow suggestions for the custom-designed system.
- ➤ Automate selectively, one function at a time. Before rolling out the whole system, conduct test runs with salespeople who are already comfortable with computers.
- ➤ Make the system easy to learn and use. Be sure to create a user-friendly interface that guides sales reps through the system. Also, the various screens should resemble the paper forms of your manual lead-tracking system.
- ➤ Provide training and support. Make sure every salesperson knows how to use the system, and provide phone support for field reps. Colombo notes that Condé Nast, the magazine publisher, broke the ice for its computer neophytes by introducing a game and a typing tutorial along with the system.

288
IDEA

Stay on Top of Sales

Effective managers must delegate, but abdication is deadly. David and Hillary Levine, owners of a construction company in Teaneck, N.J., found this out the hard way when they wanted faster growth.

They hired a part-time sales consultant who immediately hired three sales representatives and wouldn't let David accompany them on sales calls. But six months later, Hillary Levine reports: "No one sold anything, and we paid $60,000 out of pocket." Where did the Levines go wrong? A panel of experts agrees that they should have **hired just one salesperson at a time, offered performance-based incentives, and remained active in sales**.

"They were enamored with the sales manager. After hiring mine, I spent more time on the road than ever, traveling everywhere with him the first year," said Bob Evans, president of WEK Enterprises, an *Inc.* 500 clothing manufacturer in La Mirada, Calif.

"Cut the overhead—act as your own sales manager. You'll make some silly mistakes, but the goal is to figure out what the salesperson needs and point him or her in the right direction. The Levines should have passed knowledge of their niche on to a new salesperson," said Hal Fahner, a longtime sales manager now at Blue Cross/Blue Shield of Florida.

Russ Smith, managing partner of Sales and Marketing Search in Danvers, Mass., added: "The Levines chose to trust a theoretician rather than their own instincts." Stay involved and you'll see results.

SELLING • 289 • SELLING

Short and Sweet

Walk into a place looking like a salesperson, and you are going to get the big brush-off—unless you do something special," claimed Matt Hession, president of Key Medical Supply in Thibodaux, La. His strategy: **Offer potential clients a 60-second sales pitch**. Once people saw Hession take off his watch, they couldn't wait to take in his act.

To make sure busy pharmacists wouldn't say "Leave your card," or "Come back later," Hession polished a one-minute script that described the way his equipment sales and rentals worked and addressed most objections. He wanted the pharmacists to visualize the program working, without getting hung up on details.

When calling back the next week, he said, "This is Matt. I gave you the 60-second presentation." They always remembered him. 90% of them eventually signed contracts. In one year, Key Medical signed on 200 pharmacies—blanketing Louisiana—and recorded annual sales of $3 million.

290
IDEA

We'll Do Anything

When you're bootstrapping a new company, you'll do almost anything to make it succeed. Here are a few shameless **ploys to obtain new customers**.

First Team Sports, manufacturers of in-line roller skates and accessories in Mounds View, Minn., was founded on $1,000 capital. To make it look bigger, founders John Egart and David Sodequirst listed friends, wives, and distant relatives on the company information sheet and gave them titles. "We had a 'credit manager,' a 'warehouse manager,' the whole bit," Egart said. "I'd put people on hold, wait, and pick up again!"

First Team also gathered sales leads from former employers. At trade shows, Egart hovered around the Adidas booth, waiting for big customers to drop by. When they left he introduced himself and walked them down to his little booth, where his partner stood ready to pitch the line. Both founders fondly chuckle about their bootstrapping tactics, which ultimately grew First Team into a $36-million company.

Sharon's Finest, maker of tofu-based cheeses and other health foods in Santa Rosa, Calif., was founded on only $400. When Richard and Sharon Rose found a health-food store that didn't carry their product, they'd slip a note (or six) into the suggestion box, clamoring for TofuRella. Friends did the same. Eventually, they were making over $3 million in revenues, and a 5% profit.

Cooperation for a High Five

Chris MacAllister, a distributor of Caterpillar tractors in Indianapolis, thought business would improve if his managers worked more as a team at problem solving. So he designed a **bonus plan that encouraged collaboration** among his five managers and one sales director.

Bonus goals were based one-third on pretax-profit dollars, one-third on pretax-profit margin, and one-third on total sales. Profit dollars translated to what the company could put into retained earnings and profit sharing; profit margin to the managers' efficiency in running their departments, and sales volume spoke to market share. Most important, the bonus plan was an all-or-nothing proposition for the management team; they all won or they all lost.

MacAllister knew the program was working when two repeat customers gave him 100% of their business (for machines, parts, and service) after his managers teamed up on sales calls. "That wouldn't have happened if we had called on them separately," he said.

Not only did the managers meet their goals, "they blew them all away," earning bonuses approaching 50% of salary and helping the distributor emerge from an industry-wide slump. Sales jumped by 25%, to $128 million, and pretax profits rose by about 30% that year.

292

IDEA

Teach a Lesson, Gain a Customer

In the search for word-of-mouth advertisers and influencers for your business, did you ever **consider the children of your target market**? Neither did Jim Carter, co-owner of Concho Mist Water Company in San Anselmo, Texas, until a junior-high-school science teacher asked him to talk to her class about water purification.

It occurred to Carter how influential kids might be in household buying decisions. So, he agreed to take 40 students through his dealership and show them how reverse-osmosis water purification works. He had the students wash their hands in hard water, then in purified water after the minerals were extracted. It was like a magic show for the kids.

When their parents asked, "What did you learn in school today?" students must have told them about the water tour—that first demonstration resulted in four sales. Since then, Carter has received calls from other schools, and in two years the in-school demonstrations have sold 20 purification systems.

SELLING • REAL WORLD • SELLING

"My PC is my pen and paper. My voice mail is my secretary. My electronic bulletin board is my coffee break, and my fax is my car."

A RESPONDENT
to a 1995 *Inc. Technology* Fax Poll

"Several years ago, we started involving production managers in day-to-day sales and marketing decisions by having them sit in on meetings. We also sent them to trade shows. Our goal was to make sure they understood the way the work they do fits into our complete business operation and long-term goals."

JIM BAKA
president of CERAC, a specialty chemical
manufacturer in Milwaukee, Wis.

293
IDEA

Invitation to Your Booth

Frank Candy, president of the Orlando, Fla.-based American Speakers Bureau, increased awareness of his booth, and thus his trade-show sales, by 300% over the previous year by inviting his best prospects to his booth—with an incentive.

The personal invitations, which looked like greeting cards, were sent to 200 prospects one week before the show. They cost his company less than a dollar per note to produce and mail. Thirty-seven of the prospects visited his booth, representing a 19% response. He says what he used "was by far the most effective tool I've found in 15 years and hundreds of shows."

For your invitation campaign, you can purchase pre-registered attendee labels from the exposition management, or use your own list of your best prospects. **Send an incentive that necessitates a visit to your booth**, such as an offer for a personal demonstration, a free sample, or half of a two-part freebie (such as sending a key that fits a briefcase being given away at your booth).

Follow-up Payoff

According to Mark Smith, co-author of *Guerrilla Trade Show Selling* (John Wiley, 1997), qualified trade-show leads cost between $50 to $300. And yet, Smith claims, 85% of leads are never adequately followed up.

I/O Data Systems, a computer reseller in Bay Village, Ohio, doesn't make this mistake. It converts leads into paying customers by **sending booth visitors a monthly broadcast fax of sale prices**. The $2.4-million company spends about $1,000 a year on follow-up faxes and phone calls. It usually breaks even within three months of a show, says CEO Tom Tont.

Just the Fax

Harriet Donnelly, senior vice-president of Imedia, a $3.5-million marketing company in Morristown, N.J., figures that more than half of her $3 brochures were left in hotel rooms or stayed in tote bags. So, she quit handing out promotional literature at trade shows. Her alternative: **an on-site fax-back service**.

Donnelly takes notebook computers to each show, asks prospects to type their names and addresses into her database, then has them select from an on-screen form the information that interests them. Imedia faxes the material directly to the prospects' offices.

"It ends up being very, very cheap to fax something back versus having stuff thrown out," says Donnelly, who pays about $300 for a trade-show phone line and less than $1 per fax. Meanwhile, she efficiently builds a database of more qualified leads.

Since she began sending brochures only to prospects who use the fax-back service, she has cut her printing costs by one-third. After only one year and six trade shows, her database had grown to 6,000 names.

296
IDEA

Product Swap

To get exposure all over the trade show floor, **seed your product to other exhibitors for use in their booths**. Exhibitors may be willing to display your product if it helps them in booth operations, or if your product works together with theirs.

Visioneer, based in Fremont, Calif., created a buzz for its PaperPort desktop scanner at a Macintosh computer trade show in San Francisco. Several companies borrowed the PaperPort and used it to scan and capture attendee business cards or customer surveys. Some software developers demonstrated how their applications worked with the PaperPort, scanning documents and manipulating them with their image and word processors. In total, over 25 exhibitors used Visioneer's product in their booths. That trade show was the beginning of fast growth and a public offering for the company.

Power Computing, a Macintosh computer clone manufacturer exhibiting at the same show, offered its computers for exhibitors to borrow. Since most exhibitors needed a computer to demonstrate their software anyway, they gladly accepted the loan. Three years later, Power continues to use the strategy at Macintosh trade shows and has added a monitor top advertisement for its own booth. Now, almost every exhibitor at these shows uses Power's monitor or computer in his or her booth.

Put Your Trade Show on Wheels

Trade shows are great places to make friends and influence people. Carl Aschinger, CEO of Columbus Show Case, knew it was even better to **take your own show on the road**.

Aschinger, whose Ohio company made a variety of retail display cases for supermarkets, had been taking his show to customers and prospects since 1988. While he doesn't claim to have invented the idea, he did claim results.

Within his industry, a sales call led to success approximately 25% of the time. But when he began putting on his own show, Aschinger's highest rate rose to 40%. With the average trade show yielding only a 10% to 12% return, he staged his own at midpriced hotels, and it cost him 50% less.

About seven times a year a Columbus Show Case team—a salesperson, a marketing rep, and a mechanic—visit supermarket headquarters from San Francisco to Boston and Los Angeles to Tampa with a truckload of glass cases, some with fancy electronics.

"We targeted exactly who we wanted to meet," says Aschinger. "It could be the head buyer or merchandisers or the vice-presidents of construction. It's a great tool—one we'll use for many years to come."

Speech, Speech!

The rubber-chicken circuit is a great place to market your business-to-business products or services. **Get yourself featured as a speaker at trade shows, seminars, conventions, and other meetings**. As a *bona fide* expert, addressing potential customers from the podium instead of during a sales call earns you significant credibility with your audience.

It's a tactic used often by Kullman Industries, based in Avenel, N.J. The company erects buildings using modular-construction techniques. Speaking engagements allow Chuck Savage, vice president of education, to educate audiences on how these techniques are distinctive. When the time comes to sell, Savage has a better-informed and more receptive potential buyer.

Savage keeps an eye out for trade shows, exhibits, conferences, and conventions that will draw potential clients. Then he'll approach the head of the program and offer to speak on various topics. Here are Savage's dos and don'ts for a speech that will have impact:

- Talk about ideas, not about your company.
- Refer to your industry, not to your company's name.
- Educate, don't sell.

"People will hear your company's name when you're introduced," says Savage, "and afterward they'll want to talk to you. Then you're free to promote the company. Give a good speech, and you'll get your leads later."

299
IDEA

Your Own Trade Fair

Some business-to-business marketers find private shows better than big trade shows for impressing existing clients.

Once a year Synetics, a systems integrator, **hosted its own "tech fair"** in the lobby of its Wakefield, Mass., headquarters. Technology originally developed for one customer was displayed for all to view. Some 500 invitations went out to Synetics's advisers and VIP clients. "My banker always came," noted CEO Bahar Uttam, "as well as 50 to 60 customers."

Synetics's engineers staffed 21 booths, which lined the atrium lobby. "In some ways it's better than Comdex, where I had only one booth," said Uttam, who wasn't vying for foot traffic.

Though customers had come from as far as San Diego, more often the show was a local affair. Synetics also used the event as a springboard to triple business with a neighbor, Lotus Development. The tech fair complemented the few shows Synetics did attend, but it cost less than 1% of the marketing budget. What's more, the fair encouraged Synetics engineers to think real-world.

High Above the Crowd

What's the first thing customers notice at a busy trade show—your booth, your people, or your products? James C. Nelson, Jr., marketing communications manager of FWB Software, wants to make sure his hard-drive software utility products rise above trade show distractions—literally.

Before a Macintosh computer trade show in San Francisco, the $7-million company from Menlo Park, Calif., had begun shipping its new hard-drive utility software in a newly designed retail packaging. To direct people's attention to the new products, Nelson designed nine-foot replicas of the product boxes and hung them 15 feet above the booth. The boxes rotated and were brightly lit from a rented light truss. The booth was designed with the same bright color scheme as the packaging.

When it came to **corporate identification and product awareness**, the giant replicas were a great success. "Our product could be seen anywhere in the exhibit hall," exclaims Nelson. "That's often a hard task for a small software company." FWB garnered almost 3,000 leads from the show, breaking its previous show record of 1,800 leads.

Share Your Winnings

It's not easy dreaming up attention-getting promotions for trade shows. But money helps. At a conference for exposition management and meeting professionals, The Expo Group, a $12-million trade-show decorating company from Irving, Tex., announced a $500 giveaway to attendees.

Each hour during the show, for five hours, a staffer from The Expo Group held up a key that opened a locked lucite box of five $100 bills. The winning key was then dropped into a fishbowl with other similar keys, all on the same-style key chain. One by one the show managers picked out a key; and one by one each tried to open the box until the winning key turned the lock. The winner who unlocked the box received one of the $100 bills, and his or her picture was taken for the company newsletter.

After the first hour, word spread quickly that $400 was still left in the box. The show attendees started gathering around the booth—their cheers for the winner could be heard all over the hall. All this attention brought The Expo Group more than **50 qualified leads in five hours**, significantly more than the equivalent cost of a quarter-page ad in industry publications. The $500 in giveaway money turned into $300,000 worth of sales.

REAL WORLD

"When you know a guy has incredible talent but you can't harness it, you can't focus it, you can't get it into the system—it kills you."

JACK STACK
CEO of Springfield Remanufacturing Corp.

301

DO-IT-YOURSELF
MARKETING IDEAS

Other business books from *Inc.* magazine

How to *Really* Create a Successful Business Plan
How to *Really* Start Your Own Business
How to *Really* Create a Successful Marketing Plan
By David E. Gumpert

How to *Really* Deliver Superior Customer Service
Edited by John Halbrooks

The Service Business Planning Guide
The Guide to Retail Business Planning
By Warren G. Purdy

Anatomy of a Start-Up
Why Some New Businesses Succeed and Others Fail:
27 Real-life Case Studies
Edited by Elizabeth K. Longsworth

Managing People: 101 Proven Ideas for Making You
and Your People More Productive
from America's Smartest Small Companies
Edited by Sara P. Noble

301 Great Management Ideas
from America's Most Innovative Small Companies
Edited by Leslie Brokaw
with Bradford W. Ketchum, Jr.

To receive a complete listing of *Inc.* business
books and videos, please call 1-800-468-0800,
ext. 5505. Or write to *Inc.* Business Resources,
P.O. Box 1365, Dept. 5505, Wilkes-Barre, PA
18703-1365.